T0341432

THE CONSULTANT'S HANDBOOK

THE CONSULTANT'S HANDBOOK

A PRACTICAL GUIDE TO DELIVERING HIGH-VALUE
AND DIFFERENTIATED SERVICES IN A COMPETITIVE
MARKETPLACE

SAMIR PARIKH

This edition first published 2015

© 2015 Samir Parikh

Registered office

John Wiley and Sons Ltd, The Atrium, Southern Gate, Chichester, West Sussex, PO19 8SQ, United Kingdom

For details of our global editorial offices, for customer services and for information about how to apply for permission to reuse the copyright material in this book please see our website at www. wiley.com.

Wiley publishes in a variety of print and electronic formats and by print-on-demand. Some material included with standard print versions of this book may not be included in e-books or in print-on-demand. If this book refers to media such as a CD or DVD that is not included in the version you purchased, you may download this material at http://booksupport.wiley.com. For more information about Wiley products, visit www.wiley.com.

Library of Congress Cataloging-in-Publication Data
Parikh, Samir, 1970-
   The consultant's handbook : a practical guide to delivering high-value and differentiated services in a competitive marketplace / Samir Parikh.
     pages cm
   Includes index.
   ISBN 978-1-119-10620-3 (cloth)
   1. Business consultants. 2. Consulting firms–Management. I. Title.

   HD69.C6P276 2015
   001–dc23

                                                                                    2015009041

A catalogue record for this book is available from the British Library.

ISBN 978-1-119-10620-3 (hardback)
ISBN 978-1-119-10621-0 (ePub)   ISBN 978-1-119-10619-7 (ePDF)

Cover design: Wiley
Cover Image: © Andreas Rodriguez/iStockphoto
Set in 12/14 of Minion Pro Regular by SPi-Global, Chennai, India
Printed in Great Britain by TJ International Ltd, Padstow, Cornwall, UK

TABLE OF CONTENTS

ACKNOWLEDGEMENTS

With great thanks to Peter Stinner for his instrumental contributions to the development of this work.

ABOUT THE AUTHOR

Samir Parikh is a British-born consultant with over 20 years of industry experience. He began his career in the UK consulting towards the aerospace industry and then later joined a large international consulting firm where he participated in pan-European projects in the information technology, financial services and pharmaceuticals industries.

In early 2000 Samir founded SPConsulting, a global management consulting firm based in Stockholm, Sweden, specializing in organizational strategy and change management. With many of its clients being multi-national corporations, SPConsulting has conducted assignments in more than 50 countries.

The firm works closely with companies that are transforming into consulting-based organizations delivering solutions and professional services in their own areas of specialization and in highly competitive environments. Samir and his team have been responsible for helping clients to define strategies to succeed in their markets, creating new capabilities at various organizational levels and implementing maturity programmes to ensure continuous development and the maintenance of competitive advantage.

In addition to his active role as a practitioner, Samir has often been a speaker on the topic of consulting, addressing senior audiences in different industry segments as well as appearing as a guest speaker to undergraduates at leading universities and business schools.

INTRODUCTION

The objective of this book is to provide a practical context as well as tips and actionable guidelines to those working with or interested in consulting.

Suitable audiences include soon-to-be graduates interested in the consulting profession, consultants aiming to accelerate their careers through the acquisition of new ideas, and experienced practitioners wishing to complement their own experience with that of others.

Beyond the realm of consulting, the topics presented in this book could also be applied by a wide range of professionals whose roles involve frequent interactions with internal or external stakeholders, in order to improve their effectiveness and to navigate around common obstacles.

This book is designed to be easy to read, as too many consulting-related books are not. The content presented should be easy to absorb and to connect with one's own experience. The very practical approach adopted as well as a rich variety of examples are intended to make the concepts discussed easy to implement with immediate benefit in a wide range of daily situations, irrespective of the reader's experience level. The content has been organized to take the reader on a logical journey through some of the most important considerations in the practical world of consulting. Each chapter will provide a foundation for the ideas presented in the next. It is therefore recommended that the chapters are read in sequence.

Part I, *Consulting Fundamentals*, introduces some of the underlying principles that apply to any consulting-based approach. Those beginning a career in consulting should give these topics particular consideration. Mastering them with high proficiency can immediately improve the outcomes of your consulting engagements. Experienced practitioners may consider these topics as something of a review but may wish to reflect on the examples that illustrate approaches that have worked well and not so well in the past.

Part II, *Case Studies*, demonstrates how these principles can be applied successfully in consulting engagements. Three different case studies based on real industry situations are presented, providing the reader with an insight into typical daily life in consulting. The case studies are illustrated with additional content that is better presented in context than in isolation.

Part III, *Additional Topics*, explores a range of other topics that should be understood in order to gain a solid foundation of consulting knowledge. These topics include the delivery of consulting projects, the management of client-related obstacles and the skill of advising.

PART I

CONSULTING
FUNDAMENTALS

CHAPTER ONE

WHAT IS CONSULTING?

W hat is a consultant? Today many people call themselves consultants: corporations formulate their strategies with the support of management consultants; a graduate employed by an information technology (IT) company developing software is called a software development consultant; travel agencies are manned by travel consultants; gardeners call themselves landscaping consultants; and a person selling double-glazing introduces himself as a sales consultant. All of these people have quite different roles and skills. On another note, many young graduates freshly employed by companies in the consulting industry are proud of the title 'consultant' on their business card but struggle to explain to their friends and relatives from a holistic perspective exactly what it is that they do for a living.

To be successful in consulting you will need to understand its essence: What consulting is, and what it is not. This is particularly important today due to the abundant use of the consultant title. Many of the people bearing the title may not be consultants at all, or at least consulting may only constitute a small part of what they do. The unravelling of consulting and its complexities is not trivial. Consulting is a diverse activity delivered in many different contexts. We will therefore use an incremental approach to reveal the cornerstones of a consulting service as well as the obstacles and conflicts that can be associated with it.

CONSULTING: THE BASIC PROPOSITION

To begin our journey into the world of consulting, consider the following statement:

> *Consulting is a* helping *relationship provided based upon* expertise *and* experience.

Consulting is, indeed, a helping relationship and a consultant's primary focus is to help his or her client to achieve a desired objective or outcome. Helping a client may involve many different activities, according to the need and context. Advising, conducting analysis, formulating strategies, designing processes and implementing technology-based solutions are some of the most common examples of consulting help today.

The statement also suggests that the help provided by consultants is based upon two key ingredients: Expertise and experience. Together these form the basis of what we will refer to as the *basic consulting proposition*.

Consider the following example.

A client plans to build a new house and decides to employ the services of an architect. For the purposes of our discussion an architect could be considered as a type of consultant with specialist knowledge in the design and construction of buildings. Charging on an hourly basis, the architect inspects the client's plot of land and helps her to design her house. His advice is based firstly upon the expertise that he acquired in a school of architecture, and secondly upon the experience that he brings from having designed many similar buildings over the last ten years. In effect, it is the product of these two components that defines his consulting proposition: The *value* that he can deliver, and in essence the value that the client is getting for her money.

The balance of expertise and experience that forms a consultant's individual proposition can vary tremendously. A graduate new to the consulting business will usually add value based largely upon expertise or skill, such as being educated and certified in a particular business, technology-related or scientific domain. The proposition of a senior consultant, on the other hand, is more likely to be experience weighted, drawing upon the handling of diverse business situations, participation in complex projects or the findings of research accrued over a number of years. Irrespective of the balance, we have introduced the two most important variables that define a consultant's proposition, expertise and experience, which if applied effectively can result in a powerful and high-value service.

If you are working as a consultant it is important that you clearly understand your proposition as an individual. You will need to articulate it to clients and then apply it with accuracy to a variety of problems and situations. Today clients have high expectations of consultants and may challenge you, putting your proposition to the test with questions such as 'What industry certification do you have enabling you to consult in this area?' or 'How long have you worked in this solution domain? Can you give an example of a similar case that you have worked with, and the outcome?' These are fair and reasonable questions from a client, and a good consultant should be able to answer them clearly and professionally. In Chapter 3, *Establishing Credibility*, the skill of articulating the consulting proposition will be explored with a view to building a credible consultant–client relationship.

WHO IS QUALIFIED TO BE A CONSULTANT?

We have already highlighted the broad use of the consultant title. Consulting is a largely unregulated profession and, with the exception of certain specific regulated disciplines, there are usually no minimum qualifications attached to the title. Anyone who chooses to brand themselves as a consultant therefore becomes a consultant, and anyone whom a consulting company chooses to hire, albeit according to their own selection criteria, becomes a consultant. The resultant diversity of people acting in a consultant role brings with it many consequences.

Compare consulting with a strictly regulated profession, for example the accounting profession. If you want to call yourself a chartered accountant and print the title on a business card there are a number of professional exams that you must pass, even after completing a university degree. The title is protected. If you were to go to a local copy shop, print business cards bearing the title and start practising without attaining the mandatory qualifications, sooner or later the regulatory agency governing the accounting profession in your country would come along and sue you. The same principle applies to other regulated professions such as medicine. You cannot just call yourself a doctor and start practising on people. The implications would be disastrous.

In consulting there are generally no such regulations. Due to its diversity, consulting is more difficult to regulate than certain other professions and as a result a wide variety of firms and individuals present themselves to corporations as consultants. The performance of these people is generally mixed. Some may be very good, some mediocre and others may perform very badly, unable to deliver to their promises, and consequently rarely earning the opportunity to work for the same client more than once.

Consider now the impact of this dilemma from the client perspective. For clients there is a risk associated with engaging a consulting firm for the first time. The consultants may bring impressive references and present interesting proposals, but until you have seen them perform and produce results you never know exactly what you are going to get. When a client hires a chartered accountant they can be guaranteed of a basic level of skill and performance. Consulting is much more subjective, and the reputation and demonstrated track record of a consultant are therefore key to his or her success. Most well-seasoned clients can refer to at least one occasion when they had a less than satisfactory experience dealing with a consultant. In extreme cases you may encounter organizations that do not like consultants at all. If you face this situation you are likely to encounter *resistance* from client personnel based upon their scars from the past. The example below highlights one such case.

Some years ago I was flying from Newark International Airport in the United States to Stockholm, Sweden. The flight was approximately eight hours in duration and departed Newark in the early evening. The gentleman sitting next to me on the aeroplane was smartly dressed in a suit with the appearance of a senior executive. As we arrived at our seats we exchanged courtesies. During the first hours of the flight we both focused on our work, until the crew appeared to serve a meal. We placed our computers aside and engaged in light conversation over dinner. I rarely talk much about my work in such situations and generally steer towards lighter social topics of conversation.

The gentleman turned out to be a senior manager for an automotive company, based in Michigan. For many years his key area of specialization had been the design and production of heavy-duty gearboxes, a subject that he clearly relished to talk about. During the course of the next 20 minutes I learned a lot about gearboxes – everything from sensor technology to industrial lubricants and their response to different temperature gradients. My travel companion was pleasant, enthusiastic and told an interesting, although somewhat technically detailed, story.

At a certain point in the discussion the gentleman changed the subject and asked what I did for a living. I responded without hesitation, 'I am a senior consultant, working with an international firm'. The mood of our conversation changed immediately. 'Oh – a consultant!' he exclaimed with a pronounced sigh. For a moment I paused, but as usual my curiosity got the better of me. I was keen to discover what had happened to this gentleman in the not so distant past that had provoked such a reaction. 'I sense that you have some experience working with consultants', I said. 'Would you care to share it?'

His response to this question was a passionate one: 'We had some consultants working in my organization several months ago. They came in wearing dark suits. They upset all of my people doing everything their way, according to their fancy consulting methodologies. It was like an invasion. They changed a lot of things, cost us a lot of money and left us in a mess. There will definitely be no more consultants in my organization for a very long time.'

It suffices to say that the next team of consultants who engage with the organization concerned will not be welcomed with open arms by the people working there. Clients may indeed be wary regarding the value that consultants will deliver, regarding the way that they will engage, and may be haunted by past experiences. Consultants must therefore be skilled in handling negative perceptions and the obstacles associated with them. We will explore these ideas in Chapter 7, *Client Interactions and Related Obstacles.* During longer-term consulting engagements an additional client concern may relate to the consistency with which an assignment can be delivered. This is of particular relevance to larger consulting firms that may be forced periodically to rotate the resources assigned to their projects. Consider the following example.

A client engaged a team of consultants from a large, well-known firm. The consultants worked efficiently, were a pleasure to have in-house and exceeded expectations in the output that they produced. The client was delighted with the result and communicated this openly at project conclusion. The following year when another assignment was initiated, the client had no hesitation in engaging the same consulting company based upon his former experience. The second assignment was, however, carried out by a different team from the consulting company. The second team performed well but not as well, in the eyes of the client, as the first team. Although the assignment was completed successfully the client reported a lower level of satisfaction.

This situation emphasizes that consulting, like any professional service-related discipline, is a people business. Client satisfaction is highly dependent upon the skills and attitudes of the individuals carrying out the work. Consulting firms therefore need mechanisms to ensure that they can deliver with high quality and high consistency, limiting dependence on individuals.

Such mechanisms include strict recruitment criteria that go beyond educational qualifications and place a strong focus on practical and interpersonal abilities. Most firms also operate an internal certification programme tied to the defined roles within their organization. An individual aspiring to the role of senior consultant, for example, may have to demonstrate a solid base of experience as well as a highly developed skill set that meets carefully defined criteria before securing the position. It is measures such as these that enable larger firms to deliver a consistent experience to clients.

REPRESENTING A CONSULTING ORGANIZATION

If you are representing a consulting organization rather than operating as an individual, the credentials of your organization will also form an important element of your consulting proposition. When leveraged correctly, these assets become quite significant. Consider working as a consultant representing a firm of 500 people. Your consulting proposition can now be described in two parts: your personal proposition, and that of your organization. When helping your client you will be expected to:

- Leverage your own expertise and experience
- Tap into a network of 500 colleagues, locating answers to questions as needed
- Identify assets created by your organization in similar, past projects and reuse them to improve both quality and efficiency.

We can incorporate these ideas into our definition:

> *The role of a consultant is to help a client by leveraging his or her own* expertise *and* experience, *together with the* collective *expertise, experience and assets of his or her organization.*

A fundamental question is how as consultants we bring these collective assets to bear. Well-managed consulting companies are *knowledge management* companies, and a number of texts have been published on this topic. The tools and processes required to facilitate effective knowledge management vary depending upon the size of the organization as well as the types of knowledge to be managed. Both formal and informal approaches can be effective. Once, during my junior years as a consultant, a senior colleague described the importance of this with a very simple story.

'When this company started', she said, 'we were 50 employees located in one office spread over two floors of a building. If you were working on a project and needed information or an answer to a question you would consult one central resource – the coffee pot. If you went to the coffee room and chatted with colleagues you would quite easily find either someone who could answer your question, or someone who knew someone who would be able to help. The coffee pot was often something of a saviour. But now with more than 5000 employees spread across five continents the coffee pot has long since exhausted its limitations. That is why we document different types of knowledge objects in databases for easy retrieval, connect specialists globally through networks and communities, and bring people together in face-to-face events such as conferences. Knowledge management has never been more important to the competitive nature of our business'.

Larger consultancy firms invest heavily in the infrastructure required to facilitate effective knowledge management. Experience has shown, however, that the key to success is to create a knowledge sharing *culture* where employees understand the importance of both contributing to and reusing knowledge assets in their consulting assignments. Even with elaborate tools, databases and processes in place, there are still too many consulting organizations that reinvent the wheel on a daily basis. There is a tendency for creative people to follow their passion to invent before taking the time to check what has been invented before. To deliver with both high quality and high efficiency at least some form of reuse is likely to play an important role.

Many consulting firms market themselves with a great emphasis on corporate experience and knowledge capital. As a result, clients may have high expectations regarding the way in which this is leveraged during an assignment. Consider your answer to the following question if posed by a client:

> 'We selected your company due to your experience in this domain. How are you utilizing lessons learned from other cases to benefit this project and our organization?'

As a consultant representing an organisation you will need to recognize that collective knowledge is part of your proposition and incorporate this to at least some extent in each project. Clients will expect it.

ETHICS IN CONSULTING

The topic of ethics plays an important part in the shaping of the consulting proposition. Poor judgement associated with ethics has resulted in the erosion of client–consultant relationships and has been an issue in large consulting collaborations more often than one might expect. The foundation of an ethical relationship with a client relates to the helping relationship that was introduced at the beginning of this chapter.

Consultants are engaged by clients to provide help. They are expected to provide that help with the client's best interest at heart.

Consider a visit to a private doctor, a qualified and experienced medical practitioner. You pay the doctor for a premium service and expect him to give the best possible advice; to act in your best interest. The doctor makes a diagnosis and prescribes an expensive medication. A week later you find out that the doctor is being wined and dined in the city's finest restaurant by the pharmaceutical company that produces the medicine and is recommending it to everybody. You would immediately question the ethics of the decision and question whether you would ever return to the doctor, let alone recommend him to others. Questionable ethical conduct has undermined the relationship.

Providing a consulting service with the client's best interest at heart as well as respecting associated ethical practices concerning matters such as confidentiality and general conduct will usually avoid ethical dilemmas in a consultant–client relationship. The problem, however, can relate to another fundamental issue:

What is in the client's best interest and what is in the consulting company's interest to make more business may not be the same thing.

Consider the following example.

A large consulting company providing IT-related services was contracted to carry out a major systems implementation project in northern Europe. More than 100 consultants were assigned to the project for its two-year duration which represented a significant amount of revenue for the consulting company.

Everything went fine until four months before the project was due to end. Managers within the consulting company suddenly realized that soon close to 100 people would be in need of new assignments and there was little chance of developing sufficient business to maintain the high staff utilization in the time that remained. As a desperate move they approached the client to propose an extension of the project through the provision of additional services. The client was already tight on budget, but the consultants were persuasive and managed to agree an extension of the project for an additional three months, even though the proposed services were only loosely tied to the client's business priorities. Whether the extension of the project was actually in the client's best interest was somewhat questionable. Two weeks after the new work began the project was cancelled by the client as no tangible short-term benefits could be visualized. It was a less than ideal way to end a business collaboration of more than two years.

In the example above the additional services proposed had represented a way to keep the consultants busy, but with no significant benefits to the client. The consulting managers' need to sell their services overtook the key basis of a consulting collaboration, to help their customer. In large organizations managers may be under pressure to meet internal targets and a great emphasis is placed today on what is referred to as *add-on business*. Ultimately the measures defined within organizations will drive the behaviour and performance of its people. Do not, on the other hand, underestimate your clients. Sooner or later they are likely to recognize what could be referred to as *consulting overkill*. Some sceptical clients have referred to consultants as people who come into their organizations to conduct an assignment and then never leave, through success in pushing their own agendas.

So how then should consultants promote their services, meet their internal targets, and where does the correct balance lie? We will consider this question later in the chapter.

We can now incorporate the ethical dimension into our consulting definition:

> *The role of a consultant is to help a client by leveraging his or her own* expertise *and* experience *together with the* collective *expertise, experience and assets of his or her organization, acting in the client's best* interest *as a trusted adviser.*

Through the sensible application of the ideas presented, a consultancy is able to position itself as a partner and trusted adviser to a client. This requires a long-term view rather than a short-term view towards the relationship, which can be a door opener to future business as demonstrated in the example below.

A consulting firm was contacted by a small, fast-growing company working in the professional services industry. The client was concerned that their growth in employee numbers was overtaking the capability of internal business processes and had decided to embark upon a consulting initiative before the situation got out of hand. The consulting firm had been identified based upon reputation in addition to a personal referral from a member of their management team.

In an initial meeting the consultants listened to the client's requirements and concerns, assessing the activities that should be recommended and the value that could be added by a potential assignment. The issues reported by the client may have seemed challenging to the people working in the organization, but were generally not complex in nature.

The client, ready to take action, was willing to engage the consultants immediately for an initial contract period of three months.

The consultants reflected upon the case, noting that the issues were more trivial than the client had understood. Would the client later thank them for spending their money for the three months and then realizing that they could probably have solved the problem with limited help themselves? Instead of immediately accepting the assignment the consultants decided to offer some guidance. 'These are the three areas that you should focus on', they advised. 'And these are the type of actions that you should be taking. Try these recommendations, and if after three to four weeks you are still concerned we will be happy to send in a team.'

The client accepted the advice and within a month the people in the organization had successfully resolved the most critical issues themselves.

A year later the consultants were contacted by the client again, regarding a new, much larger opportunity. Based upon the credibility that had been created in the first interaction they were engaged directly, without consideration of other potential consulting suppliers.

Engaging as a partner means having the best interest of your client at heart. As in a personal relationship, you sometimes favour the interest of your partner over your own short-term gains as an investment in a longer-term, valuable relationship. In the practical world of consulting this may mean that not every new client discussion results in immediate business for the consultancy, but that every action you take constitutes a positive next step in your relationship with that client. Demonstrating this intention not only through your words but also through your actions can result in strong client relationships that may shield you from competitors and be your ticket to a long-term business partnership.

CONSULTING VERSUS SELLING

> A landscape gardening consultant has appointments with two new clients one Saturday. He tends to arrange such meetings on Saturdays as it is easy to get face time with clients and discuss their options for realizing a variety of garden transformations. He has been in the business for more than 25 years.
>
> He inspects the first client's garden and recommends the trimming of some tall spruce trees, reshaping of the lawn and the replacement of the garden fence despite the fact that the existing fence is in fair condition and could simply be repainted. The landscape gardener's brother happens to be a carpenter who makes fences. The gardener often sells fencing to his clients and gets a good commission from his brother. The client eventually agrees to the plan and a deal is closed.
>
> His second visit is to an old mansion undergoing a full renovation. The garden has not been tended for years and is overgrown. Remains of an old wooden fence, hardly visible in places, separate the garden from neighbouring woodland. The gardener eagerly recommends a new fence to the client to cover the entire perimeter. 'Yes, agrees the client. You are quite right. Deer stray in from the woodland and eat anything that we try to grow here'. Once again a deal is closed.

Consulting and selling are different things. They have different objectives or *agendas*, although many people and organizations are required to do both. The objective of consulting is to help the client, acting in the client's best interest. The objective of selling is to persuade the client to buy your product or service and to do whatever you can to make a deal. A car dealer will try to sell you a vehicle from his brand at a premium price, even if he knows that another vehicle from a competing brand would provide what you need for less money. His agenda is not to advise and act in your best interest, but to make a sale.

In our landscape gardener example, when meeting the first client the gardener was not consulting with regard to the new fence, he was selling. He understood that the existing fence could have been repainted but seized the opportunity to sell a new one, under the guise of consulting and providing advice. The proposition put forward was not in the client's best interest but represented a way for the vendor to make business and in this case a commission. When meeting the second client, however, he was consulting, even if inadvertently. The advice that he provided was in the client's best interest. It was easy for the client to recognize this and the advice was therefore easily accepted.

How should consultants sell their services?

So how should consultants sell their services? The answer, quite simply, is by identifying where the services or solutions that they can provide coincide with the client's needs and best interests. Consider the following example.

Figure 1.1 represents a consulting firm's portfolio containing various services and solutions. Depicted by letters, these could include various types of analyses, feasibility studies, process improvement initiatives, automation solutions, the collection and reporting of metrics, and so forth.

Figure 1.2 adds, through well-informed discussions with the client, the scope of the client's actual needs. As the diagram illustrates, some of the services in the consulting portfolio are relevant to the client's needs whereas others are not.

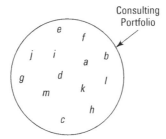

Figure 1.1: A consulting portfolio

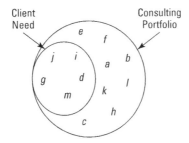

Figure 1.2: A client's need

Figure 1.3 therefore suggests an optimal approach for the consultancy to promote its services. In the area where the consulting portfolio and the client's legitimate needs coincide, promoting additional services could be regarded as *partnering*. In essence,

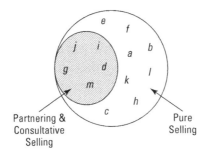

Figure 1.3: Partnering opportunities

you are seeking additional ways to help your client according to their needs and best interests. In the area where the consulting portfolio and the client's needs do not coincide, the promoting of any services or solutions is a pure selling exercise. As in our landscape gardener example, you may be persuasive enough to close a deal, but in the long run your client is likely to realize that your services were over-sold, which will have consequences on your continued relationship.

This distinction is one of the cornerstones of *consultative selling*, an approach that is employed in many industries today. Instead of presenting their portfolios, consultants seek to understand their clients' business needs and then selectively propose offerings to accurately address those needs, which in turn is more likely to be welcomed by clients. The approach is also closely aligned with the add-on sales directives within consulting companies that seek to grow their business within a client by identifying new opportunities and presenting propositions for additional work. Some may consider this type of upselling inappropriate, but many clients have the opposite perception provided that the upselling is done in an appropriate manner. This was exemplified by the comment below made by a senior operations manager working in the telecommunications industry.

'Good consultants demonstrate proactive behaviour. Some of the consultants that we use are actually better qualified than we are to spot excellent opportunities for us to improve things in a way that benefits our organization. What we want is for them to approach us, saying "have you considered that changing this process and conducting this analysis would result in the following business benefits?" The worst thing that we could possibly say is "no thanks". Consulting vendors just deliver what you asked for. A consulting partner is in the boat with you, thinking ahead with you, and trying to help you. This is the type of relationship that we want with consultants – if they are not being proactive they are not behaving as a partner.'

CHAPTER SUMMARY

This chapter has discussed the following points:

- The role of a consultant is to help a client by leveraging his or her own expertise and experience together with the collective expertise, experience and assets of the consulting organization, acting as a trusted adviser with the client's best interests at heart.

- Consulting is a largely unregulated profession, and many people call themselves consultants. We must therefore be accurate in the way that we set client expectations, in the way that we articulate our propositions, and in the way that we describe what we can deliver. Otherwise clients may expect us to work in the same way as the last people that they engaged called 'consultants'.

- Clients may have negative perceptions based upon the scars of past consulting experiences, which may in turn translate into obstacles within new consulting collaborations. As consultants we will need to be skilled in managing such obstacles and perceptions.

- Consulting is a people business, and the skills and attitudes of the assigned team will have a definite impact on the client experience. Larger consulting firms require mechanisms to ensure consistency amongst the resources that they provide to clients.

- Knowledge management is an important internal function in any consulting organization in order to achieve both quality and efficiency. Avoid reinventing the wheel. Experience has shown that the first step to becoming a knowledge-sharing organization is to create a knowledge-sharing culture.

- Consulting and selling are different activities with different agendas. When promoting your services, act as a partner by employing a consultative selling-based approach.

- Identifying a consulting proposition that is in the client's interest is essential to an ethical consulting collaboration.

When evaluating a new consulting opportunity, consultants should ask themselves the questions: Can we provide a solution to this problem? And is our intended solution in the client's best interest?

- Clients often expect proactivity as part of a consulting relationship. Consider how you can further help your client by leveraging the capabilities of your organization, and how this may translate into new business opportunities.

CHAPTER TWO

PREPARING TO CONSULT

Consulting is not delivered in a vacuum but rather towards a specific context: that of a client or client organization. Each client situation is unique and a good understanding of your client must be combined with the associated inputs, requirements and the expertise and experience of the consultancy to produce an effective consulting solution.

Think, for example, of a doctor consulting a patient. The doctor will try to learn as much as possible about the patient by reviewing medical records and conducting an examination. He will capture inputs in terms of symptoms or complaints by means of a carefully constructed dialogue and then finally apply his expertise and experience to recommend the course of action that is most suitable to the patient's situation. The treatment advice provided to different patients, even those with similar symptoms, could vary considerably depending on a number of situational factors.

To consult effectively requires an approach tailored, at least somewhat, to the client context. The better you understand your client, the more likely you will be able to provide a solution that will be effective. As in our doctor example, it is not uncommon to encounter two businesses experiencing quite similar challenges, yet the optimal solution approach may be different in each case due to factors such as the organization's structure, decision-making processes, internal culture and the local market situation. In short, we need to understand some basic factors about our clients before we can consult effectively. This will require some preparation.

The topic of preparation could be considered as a critical point in consulting maturity. All too often, consultants engage with clients without sufficient preparation, boasting about industrialized solutions and what they have achieved in projects elsewhere rather than respecting the unique situation of each client and adapting their approach accordingly. Whilst requiring less effort, this short-cut is a risky one that may result in compromised client benefits as well as potentially undermining the credibility of the consultants.

Client expectations also play an important role. Clients expect us to be prepared and to address them intelligently in the context of their business and industry. Most clients can spot immediately who is well prepared and who is working from a blank sheet of paper, a mechanism that allows them to judge very early in an engagement the calibre of the consultancy and the applicability of the advice that is likely to follow. In the competitive world of consulting, this should be considered as a point of differentiation. If your competitor is better prepared and more client-oriented than you are, then you may easily be outperformed.

Naturally we would always like to engage in a well-prepared manner, but a practical limitation that we may often face is time. What should you do if you are asked to meet a new client at short notice? In this chapter we will classify preparation activities into three types: *Basic preparation, detailed preparation* and *engagement-specific preparation*. These will be combined into a scalable approach that maximizes the value of preparation efforts relative to the time available. Clear guidelines will be presented, but these should not be considered exhaustive and may need to be adapted to the field of consulting in which you are working.

BASIC PREPARATION

Basic preparation addresses the 'must know' elements before engaging in a credible discussion with a client. Some of the most common basic preparation elements are suggested in Figure 2.1, which could be considered as a checklist. The number of elements is limited intentionally as it should be feasible to collect this information in just one to two hours. Each item is elaborated in the paragraphs below. If you are asked to attend a client meeting at short notice, this would be the type of preparation that you might attempt in the limited time available.

Industries of operation, geography, headquarters The industries that the client is addressing (e.g. consumer electronics, healthcare, insurance), geographical scope covered, headquarters and office locations. If the client has any overseas holdings or ownership in other businesses this may also be relevant.

Financials (in brief) The revenue and profit reported for the last financial year, if published. The amount of money

COMPANY INFORMATION

Industries of operation
Geography (offices and presence)
Headquarters location
Financials (in brief)
Key executives
Business units
Market position, key competitors
News and press releases

PORTFOLIO OFFERING & CUSTOMERS

Product and service offering
Customers and customer segments

INTERNAL INTELLIGENCE

Previous projects and their outcomes
Known issues or needs
Existing contacts and relationships

Figure 2.1: Basic preparation elements

that a business is making is likely to affect the way that budgets are allocated and the appropriate ambition level of a consulting solution. In some cases, consultants have presented 'Rolls Royce' style solutions to clients who are making little money, clearly without success. Through preparation this feedback could have been anticipated and a more suitable approach pursued.

Key executives   Know the names of the top executives in the client organization. When clients refer to these individuals in discussions you should not look blank or need to ask 'Who is Mr. Joyce?'

Business units   If a company is divided into business units, this is something to be aware of. This may also affect the scope of the consulting initiative.

Market position, key competitors   Competitive position, rank in the industry, market share and key competitors. This information is generally obtained from analyst reports and public (published) analyses.

News and press releases   May relate to a wide variety of topics such as international expansion, partnerships, acquisitions, the divesting of non-profitable entities, and so forth.

Product and service offering   Understand the products or services that your client is providing to customers and the way in which the offering is structured and priced.

Customers and segments addressed   What types of customers does your client do business with and which customer segments are of interest?

Particularly for consultancies conducting recurrent business with larger client organizations, internal intelligence will play an important role. This may relate to previous projects and their outcomes, known issues or needs, business priorities, sensitivities, internal politics and decision-making culture. Existing relationships should be considered and may need to be leveraged.

Assimilation of these basic preparation elements should be considered essential prior to conducting an informed client dialogue.

DETAILED PREPARATION

If you are to be assigned to a client account for a longer period of time and if more time is available for preparation, you may wish to extend your efforts into what we will refer to as *detailed preparation*. The level of detail incorporated could be quite exhaustive; however, the additional items suggested in Figure 2.2 provide a good starting point, typically extending the total preparation time to between a half day and a day.

Strategy: Vision and objectives   What are the client's stated business vision and strategic objectives? This information will affect the definition of business priorities. Ultimately you may need to explain how any consulting proposition is

COMPANY INFORMATION

Strategy: vision and objectives
Company history
Notable industry trends

PORTFOLIO OFFERING & CUSTOMERS

New products and services
Sales channels
Marketing and positioning strategies
Customer references and testimonies

FINANCIAL INFORMATION

Revenues
Profit
Cash flow
Business unit performance

Figure 2.2: Detailed preparation elements

aligned to the corporate vision in order to gain support. This type of information can often be found on the client's website or in the introductory section of the most recent annual report.

Company history   An awareness of key milestones in the history of your client can provide a valuable insight into its decision-making culture, particularly if there have been mergers and acquisitions.

Notable industry trends   Review articles about the industry and understand what analysts are saying about the future. Points for consideration may include future growth opportunities, the impact of new technologies, changes in regulation or shifts in the competitive landscape.

New products and services   Has your client recently launched any new products or services, and what has been the uptake? These could be hot topics of conversation.

Sales channels   How does your client sell its products or services? Does it manage a sales force, use third-party brokers, own branded stores or sell through franchising?

Marketing and positioning strategies Some clients employ an aggressive marketing approach. Others may be more traditional. Positioning refers to the way in which the client business presents itself to the market and the values with which it aims to be associated. Some companies, for example, aim to be associated with a low price perception, whilst others may associate themselves with high quality or leading-edge innovation. Understanding these strategies will give you a valuable insight into the client's business model and related priorities.

Customer references and testimonies Some companies publicize customer references and success stories as proof points demonstrating the value that they can deliver. Familiarize yourself with these.

Financials Examine the financials of the client's business in detail. If the organization is divided into business units, what is the financial contribution of each? Pay close attention to trends: are revenues increasing or decreasing compared to the last financial reporting period? Examine the relationship between revenue and profit. If profits are stable or increasing but revenue is static or declining, then increases in profit will be the result of cost-cutting initiatives. The client may therefore need help to grow the top line of their business. If, on the other hand, revenues are increasing without proportional increases in profit, discussions may need to focus on cost reduction, outsourcing and automation.

Assimilation of these detailed preparation elements will provide a more thorough overview of the client's business and the surrounding context.

ENGAGEMENT-SPECIFIC PREPARATION

Engagement-specific preparation is reserved for the common situation when a client invites you to meet in order to discuss

THE CLIENT DISCUSSION

Topic of discussion and agenda
Participating stakeholders
Basis established so far
Anticipated questions from the client
Questions to ask, inputs required
Related consultancy experience

Figure 2.3: Engagement-specific preparation elements

a specific topic. Whilst basic and detailed preparation relate to the client's business, engagement-specific preparation relates to the specific topic or issue to be discussed. Consideration of the elements listed in Figure 2.3 will generally ensure that you are prepared.

Topic of discussion   What are the agreed topics of discussion, and has an agenda been agreed in advance? In the absence of an agenda, which topics should be covered for the discussion to be productive?

Participating stakeholders   Who will you be meeting from the client organization? What are their backgrounds and probable expectations? Are all stakeholders likely to be positive towards the discussion or is any resistance anticipated?

Basis established so far?   If this is not the first meeting with the client to discuss the topic, review the basis that has been established so far and the logical next steps in the discussion.

Anticipated questions from the client   Consider questions that the client is likely to ask and that you may need to answer. Do some homework in advance and prepare answers, backed up with references or examples if needed. This type of preparation will improve your ability to perform well in front of the client.

Questions to ask, inputs required   List the questions that you may need to ask in order to obtain a clear understanding of the client's requirements. Consider any unknowns or assumptions that may need to be clarified in order to proceed efficiently after the meeting.

Related consultancy experience   Which other projects have been conducted by your consulting company in this area? Which references can be presented (if requested) and what experience could be reused? Clients place a high emphasis on reference cases during early discussions.

Resources

A wide range of information resources can be used to support preparation activities. Some of the most common are listed below.

The client's website   Usually a good resource for information such as corporate vision, strategic objectives, corporate values, product and service offering, organization and geography.

Press releases   Provide a wide variety of information such as recent events, new initiatives, partnerships, acquisitions and organizational changes.

Annual reports   Provide financial information (income statement, balance sheet, cash flow statement) as well as an introductory account on general performance and progress in the execution of the organization's strategy. This is typically very insightful information.

Analyst reports and industry analysis   Can be very useful in understanding industry trends, market expectations, competitive threats and potential opportunities.

(Internal) knowledge management databases   Most consulting firms maintain knowledge management databases containing information on their clients, past projects, their outcomes, and reusable assets.

Internet searches   Can provide a large amount of information on people, business transactions and references, some of which should be regarded with caution unless published by a reliable source.

Contacts and colleagues   Colleagues within your organization or network who have worked with the client before may be able to share very useful advice and information. Particularly in consulting organizations conducting recurrent business with a client, this may be a very important resource.

CHAPTER SUMMARY

As consultants we are required to address a wide range of business issues efficiently, yet in many cases consultants engage without sufficient preparation. Ask yourself the question whether you have ever engaged with a client without a basic grip on the elements presented in this chapter.

Clients have high expectations, and therefore insufficient preparation may put you in an awkward situation. Furthermore, poor preparation may sacrifice a good opportunity to perform well in front of the client, discussing issues clearly and accurately in the correct business context.

A simple but scalable approach has been presented in this chapter classifying preparation into three types. Together with the intelligent use of information resources, these can be used to maximize the value created by preparation efforts relative to the time available.

- **Basic preparation** Can be executed quickly and captures the 'must know' elements before engaging in a credible discussion
- **Detailed preparation** An extension of basic preparation, useful in preparing for longer-term engagements with a client (e.g. prior to embarking on a consulting assignment) and when more time is available
- **Engagement-specific preparation** Relates to a specific discussion, topic or issue, and performed in order to ensure an efficient approach and valuable outcome.

CHAPTER THREE

ESTABLISHING CREDIBILITY

The skill of establishing credibility is fundamental to anyone working in a consulting-related profession. Clients generally decide whether to accept advice based upon two factors: The basis and quality of the advice itself; and the credibility of the organization or people presenting the advice. Our credibility influences the relationships that we are able to build with clients, the level of cooperation that we are able to secure and the way that we are perceived relative to other consulting providers.

In Chapter 1 we introduced the idea of the consulting *proposition* that describes the value that we are able to bring to the table as consultants. When meeting new clients you will need to articulate the basis of your proposition. Usually delivered in the form of a simple introduction, this in itself is a skill. If delivered proficiently, the client should understand the areas that you can be consulted on, the capabilities that you possess and your potential contributions.

> *In consulting you must know and be able to articulate your proposition. Without a proposition that is understood by your client you will not be able to consult effectively.*

So how do we position ourselves, or even our colleagues, through a credible introduction? Consider the following personal introduction statements.

Example 1

'I would like to introduce John Smith. He is a consultant from our finance industry practice and brings broad financial experience to this project. He is one of our best consultants and I am sure that you will be very satisfied with his contributions.'

Example 2

'May I introduce Stuart Jones? Stuart is a consultant from our finance industry practice and brings nine years of experience working with risk management solutions.'

Example 3

'Please meet Damon Jarvis. Damon brings nine years of experience as a consultant in our finance industry practice, working specifically with risk management solutions. We selected him for this engagement as he has just returned from a similar project in South America with one of the leading banks there.'

Which consultant would you engage: John, Stuart or Damon? The three statements could, in the absence of names, have referred to the same person, yet each positions the individual quite differently and with a different resulting client perception.

POSITIONING: THE PERSONAL INTRODUCTION

The word *positioning* refers to the way that we present ourselves as professionals and the client perception that is created as a result. There is an art to positioning oneself and creating an appropriate perception through a good introduction, yet many skilled people fail to articulate their propositions clearly. As a result, their potential contributions are not understood and they are not leveraged by their clients in the most valuable way.

The following characteristics should be given due consideration when making an introduction at the individual level.

Objective

A credible introduction is an objective one. As consultants we avoid 'selling' ourselves, beating our chests and saying how good we are. Most mature clients would simply roll their eyes and think 'here comes yet another superman!' Still worse is the phenomenon of overselling. Presenting an exaggerated view of capabilities can lead to the setting of unrealistic expectations that become difficult or impossible to satisfy. Instead the style that we adopt when introducing ourselves as consultants is one of *presenting evidence*. The factual evidence that we present in an introduction provides the client with a clear basis to make their own evaluation of who we are and the potential contributions that we can make. Let us consider our three examples again.

Example 1 is vague, rather selling-oriented and would fail to impress most clients. Clients have met too many consultants who brag about themselves, often in the absence of a solid experience base. The words 'he is one of our best' are risky and unwise. We are all human, and the first time that John makes a mistake the reputation of his organization will take a direct hit. 'And he was supposed to be one of your best...', the client will say.

Tangible

An introduction that is too vague or fluffy is likely to be ineffective. A more tangible approach is achieved by *quantifying* the consultant's expertise and experience. Expertise in a specialist field or technology could be quantified by reference to certification by a recognized body. Experience can be quantified by specifying the number of years in a specific domain or through the use of references to similar work that was conducted successfully elsewhere.

To this end Example 2 offers much more clarity. The years of experience are quantified as a substitute for the phrase 'broad experience'. Such phrases are general in nature and somewhat weak, yet are commonly heard in introductions. Additionally, the domain of experience is now more precisely stated. Example 1 told us that the consultant belonged to a finance industry practice, which may address a very diverse set of issues. This time a more specific reference to risk management solutions is included. The client can now begin to understand what this individual can actually do, the problems that he can solve, and the questions that he can be approached with. The consulting proposition provided by the individual is now beginning to emerge.

Example 3 further quantifies the value of practical experience by including a reference. References tend to command a high level of attention from clients, as staff with hands-on experience understand the obstacles and issues that are likely to arise during the execution of consulting projects and are familiar with strategies for overcoming them.

Relevant

When making an introduction it is your responsibility to connect your skills and experience to the discussion context and the needs of your client. This requires you to consider the experience that you have built up over time, to identify the most relevant points to the situation at hand and to emphasize them. This is very different from reciting a standard introduction to different clients time after time. Ask yourself the questions: Which of my skills are most relevant to this situation? What similar work have I done in the past and how can that experience be leveraged? Having heard your introduction, you would like the client to think 'It will be great to have this person on the team. His skills and experience will be extremely valuable.'

Concise

The ability to communicate concisely and deliver clear, emphatic content in a few words is an admirable quality of a skilled speaker. Coupled with the prudent selection of vocabulary, it can be very powerful.

Consider the length of your introduction and the amount of content to include. If you are to be the main speaker at a one-day seminar it may be pertinent to spend two to three minutes outlining your experience, enabling participants to draw upon it and direct questions appropriately. In a meeting, on the other hand, when participants make short round-the-table introductions you may need to restrict yourself to a just a few words.

'Stuart Jones, 20 years working in telecommunications with a focus on operational processes and automation...'

Even in a few words it is usually possible to articulate clearly the nature and depth of your experience, building credibility and outlining your potential contributions.

POSITIONING: THE CORPORATE INTRODUCTION

Having introduced the members of the consulting team, consider whether you need to present the proposition of your organization as a whole. Organizational assets also constitute an important part of your proposition, but careful consideration will be needed with regard to your approach and the time taken to present them. Avoid turning the dialogue into a lengthy company presentation unless this has been specifically requested. 'Organizational accolades are important', clients often say, 'but really it is the team that you get who will make the difference.'

> A consulting company employed the general practice of including a few introductory slides describing references and corporate capabilities at the beginning of each client presentation. This material, whilst potentially interesting to first-time clients, was rather standard in nature. When one such presentation was delivered to a client in the Middle East several minutes were spent covering the introductory slides. When the consultants then moved on to the main topic of discussion, the client remarked: 'Now finally the selling is over. Let's get down to business!'

As this example illustrates, a delicate balance is required. Of course we want the client to understand our corporate credentials, but too great an emphasis on this will result in the perception of selling. A technique that can be used to achieve this balance is to provide the client with what is informally referred to as a *hook*. Having introduced the individuals at the table, the consultant leading the dialogue may make a statement such as:

> *'Clearly our company brings significant experience in the logistics industry related to automation solutions. Would you like to hear more about our references, or should we move on to discuss the issue at hand?'*

What you are doing is giving the client an option to decide whether they want to hear about your company's background and references at this point. Experience suggests that nine out of ten clients generally decline the offer, stating that references can be provided later in documented form, and are more interested in continuing to the main discussion. In some cases, however, your client may be curious, latch on to the hook, and ask a specific question such as, 'Do you have any references in the area of warehouse management automation?' Have your reference material on stand-by and be prepared to answer such questions if they come up.

The competitive aspect of positioning

Consulting is a highly competitive business, and clients often invite multiple firms to tender for assignments. As we have suggested, the careful selection of appropriately skilled resources to form a consulting team is an important point of evaluation for a client. Clear articulation of such capabilities during the introduction can create a tactical advantage over competitors and should not be underestimated.

Two large consulting firms – Company A and Company B – were competing for a large consulting assignment. They were invited to a common meeting by the potential client to present their views on the optimal solution approach. Each firm sent five representatives to the meeting.

When the representatives from Company A made their introductions they were professional although somewhat brief, introducing themselves with titles such as 'senior consultant', 'project manager' and 'solution architect'. Some referred to a specific domain of expertise, others did not. When the representatives from Company B introduced themselves, they had clearly considered in advance exactly what each person was going to say. They had identified the exact experience that should be emphasized in the context of each consultant's role, together with previous project references that should be mentioned.

This proved to be an effective and tactical move. Although both firms had substantial experience in the domain, the second firm was perceived to be better qualified due to the clarity with which its representatives had positioned themselves.

CHAPTER SUMMARY

Credibility is fundamental to anyone working in a consulting-related role. As consultants we regularly meet with new stakeholders and we are required to build credibility quickly. Establishing credibility is also the first step in the client relationship building process.

- The building of credibility usually starts with the clear articulation of an individual's consulting proposition in the form of a personal introduction. This should not be regarded as a selling exercise, but rather a process of presenting credentials and evidence.

- An effective personal introduction should be *objective, tangible, relevant* and *concise*. Vague terms or statements should be avoided. Consider the words that you will use to introduce yourself next time you meet a new client. What expertise and experience makes you qualified to address your audience on the topic? How can it be articulated? How can it be quantified? Should the broader assets of your organization be referred to?

- If you are competing for a consulting assignment, consider the competitive aspect of positioning carefully. If you are perceived to be better positioned for the work than your competitors, it will provide you with a clear advantage.

- If you are a graduate applying for a consulting position, consider how you will build credibility at an interview. 'Could you tell us something about yourself?' is a common opening question. How will you combine your personal, academic and extracurricular background into a concise, interesting and relevant account?

Two consultants who applied the techniques described in this chapter for the first time made the following observations. The first consultant had been tasked with the delivery of a presentation to a group of client executives in Australia.

'It was very interesting. I tried out some of the techniques related to positioning. I spent a little more time introducing myself than I would usually do, and included more specific references with respect to my experience. The clients paid much more attention than usual, and asked some very interesting questions.'

The second consultant referred to a client meeting that she had participated in as part of a consulting team in North America.

'I was the only one to make a good introduction of myself at the beginning of the session, and I received the most questions!'

CHAPTER FOUR

MANAGING CLIENT MEETINGS

The ability to engage with clients in an *efficient* and *accurate* manner is important to the success of any consulting assignment.

Much of our engagement with clients takes place in the form of meetings. Meetings may concern the discussion of new opportunities, the joint formulation of approaches and strategies, the reporting of progress during project delivery and a wide range of other themes. The approach and style with which consultants engage has a great impact on the client experience. This was highlighted by a senior marketing executive working in the airline industry.

> We work with a number of consulting firms and marketing agencies. Each firm brings its own specialist focus area; however, our experience of working with them can be quite different. When we issue a brief some firms come and meet with us and ask questions about the brief. We provide our answers and then the consultants return to their office to work on it. Four days later they call us and set up another meeting to ask additional, more detailed questions. We collaborate in this way, but it takes about three iterations and perhaps two weeks before they are able to deliver a draft that is appealing and close to what we want. Other firms can be quite different. Their people come in extremely well prepared. They ask us very good questions related to the brief, sometimes questions that we had not even considered ourselves. Then after just one meeting they are able to submit an initial proposal that meets our needs quite closely.

The two experiences described by this executive are very real in the world of consulting. A conscious and disciplined decision is required: are we going to engage with our clients accurately and efficiently, or take the run-in–run-out consulting approach?

The issues that we work with in consulting are generally complex, and therefore a *structured approach* will be required to arrive at a successful outcome efficiently, navigating to the most critical discussion points and avoiding a long, unstructured or circular dialogue. It is the role of a consultant to ensure that the discussion is well structured, and we cannot rely on our clients for this. Another idea that will be equally important is that of *flexibility*. A meeting with a client is a two-way vehicle and needs to embrace the inputs and expectations of the client, not only the discussion points that the consultants wish to raise. Some of these expectations may be unpredictable. Mechanisms can be applied to achieve this flexibility through the use of *check points* and what we will refer to as *navigation*.

This chapter will explore the steps required to prepare for and direct a client meeting, driving it efficiently towards an accurate outcome, in particular:

- The setting of meeting objectives
- Composing the consulting participant team
- Agreeing on a team plan
- Structuring the interaction
- The post-meeting debrief.

In Part II of this book we will demonstrate how these ideas can be applied in practice using real-life case studies.

SETTING THE MEETING OBJECTIVES

The success of any meeting, whether conducted internally or together with a client, depends upon how well you are able to meet your intended meeting objectives.

Consider how people evaluate the success of the meetings that they participate in. They are often influenced by factors such as the number of positive agreements that have been reached, the level of interest that has been demonstrated by clients or colleagues, the number of questions that have been asked when a new concept is presented, or follow-on steps and commitments that have been made. Whilst these are relevant indicators, in consulting a more precision-based approach is required. It is not sufficient to walk into a meeting armed with an agenda and see what will happen. Instead we define a set of *meeting objectives* in advance, we structure our approach according to them, and after the meeting we measure our success relative to them. In practice you will rarely have more than five key objectives for a meeting, and three or four objectives is more common. The process of setting meeting objectives should be a formal one. When working as a consulting team it is worthwhile to agree on your objectives and write them down during preparation.

Experience has shown that this makes a positive difference. If everyone has the same view of the objectives they will pull in the same direction during the meeting. If something is being missed or overlooked, someone will step in and take action. Formal agreement of objectives provides the basis for improved teamwork.

COMPOSING THE CONSULTING PARTICIPANT TEAM

Having defined the objectives of your meeting, your next consideration will be to assemble the team that you will need in place to meet them.

The team that you send to meet with a client constitutes an important part of your engagement approach. Clients have remarked that it is interesting to observe how the approach varies between consulting companies, some sending in one or two consultants and others trying to impress them with a small army of people. Consulting companies consider this question in reverse. Should they send in one or two people and risk creating a perception of being underqualified, or should they send a larger team, some of whom will listen silently but with no opportunity to contribute? This is one of the many situations where good judgement is required. Your decision should be driven by the purpose and duration of the meeting, the expertise required at the table to achieve the desired outcome, the number of client participants attending, and in some cases cultural expectations.

The advantage of engaging with a larger team, four or five participants for example, is that it provides a clear demonstration of the competence at hand to address the issue, provided of course that the participants are clearly introduced and able to play an active role. The weight of the impression that this makes should not be underestimated. Consultancies usually tell their clients that they have 'many well qualified people with suitable expertise', but when the client actually gets to meet these consultants the proof is delivered. Engaging with a larger team, however, can also bring with it some disadvantages. The meeting will immediately become more complex to manage, and time can quickly slip away as everyone wants to have their say. You will need to appoint a chairperson on the consultant side to coordinate the flow of communication and keep things on track. The chairperson will usually open the meeting, close the meeting and direct the client's questions to the most appropriate person on the team. Bringing a larger team to a short meeting also means that some team members may never really get the chance to contribute at all. In this case the client may wonder why they attended.

The number of participants attending a meeting has a definite impact on client perception. Experience suggests that a leaner approach is generally better and achieved by sending a few well-prepared participants, as illustrated in the example below.

Three consulting companies in North America were invited by a client to a one-day workshop to discuss upcoming changes in regulatory issues. The first company, a large consultancy, sent six representatives to the workshop. The second company sent four and the third company, a small firm, sent only two consultants. As the day progressed it emerged that the two representatives from the small company were very well prepared. They managed to answer all of the questions just as well as the large firm did with its team of six. At the conclusion of the day the client approached the large firm, thanked them for their participation, but commented 'Sending in a team of six, we can understand why you are generally quite expensive...'

When a consultancy engages with a larger team it is usually a move to ensure that any question put forward can be answered. Keep in mind that your aim is to be well prepared to discuss the agreed topics, and a smaller team can usually handle this. Questions that are more advanced or beyond the expected scope of the meeting can be taken off-line and dealt with as action items.

The contrasting views presented above illustrate different but highly relevant considerations. The team that you assemble will directly impact the dynamics of the discussion as well as the client's experience of engaging with you. Pick your participants carefully. Do not bring Bob to the meeting if Bob is not needed but you feel that Bob will feel left out, and do not walk around the office half an hour before a meeting saying 'We are going to the client, who's coming along?' Poor practices result in poor performance.

AGREEING ON THE TEAM PLAN

Having assembled the consultant team, you will need a team plan before engaging with the client.

As a team you would like to perform in front of your client like a well-oiled machine. As in any other team situation, such as playing a baseball game, you will therefore need to put a team plan in place. The level of formality and time required to do this may vary quite considerably, depending on the consulting team and the complexity of the intended client discussion. For a team of three consultants who work frequently and fluidly together it may be sufficient to get together informally over a cup of coffee and discuss the game plan. A larger team, on the other hand, planning a full-day workshop to discuss a complex issue with a client that may have objections and concerns may need to spend a few hours working out their strategy. But in both situations the team will need to align and adopt a common position on the way in which the meeting will be approached.

Agreement will be required on the following items, which could be considered as a simple checklist:

Roles Who will do what? Everyone should be engaged and have a role to play, whether their contribution is to present, to collect requirements or to assist in the answering of questions. Decide who will act as the chairperson and manage the flow of the meeting as a whole and who will lead each discussion point on the agenda.

How questions will be handled Avoid the situation where the client asks a question and three consultants leap forward to answer at the same time. A common practice is to agree that the person who is leading the point under discussion will be the first in line to respond to questions and then the other team members will support with their views as necessary. Questions that do not relate to a specific discussion point are often addressed by the chairperson and further directed, if necessary, to an appropriate member of the consulting team.

Commitments to be made or avoided Consideration of these items in advance can avoid awkward moments in the discussion. In your preparation meeting you may agree, for example, 'Even if the client pushes us we will not provide a cost estimate today. All requirements must be gathered first' or 'We will not discuss the solution details today. We are not prepared for this. If questions come up we will propose a separate workshop to address them later on.'

Note-taking Good note-taking is an important skill for consultants who aim to address their client's needs with accuracy and attention to detail. Typically all of the consultants present will record notes during the discussion. This not only provides you with a valuable record of the discussion, but also demonstrates active listening towards the client. Some clients have been critical of consultants who simply sit and nod during a meeting: 'Why are we providing all of this information, when clearly nobody is taking it on board?'

It is also advisable to appoint a 'chief note-taker' in advance, a responsibility that is often rotated within the team. This individual will make sure that they take good and well-structured notes and will be responsible for the end-of-meeting summary as well as the publication of meeting minutes.

STRUCTURING THE INTERACTION

With the team assembled and a team plan in place, you now need to decide how to structure the meeting interaction.

A structured interaction approach will be essential to gain the most out of the meeting opportunity. At the same time the approach should be as simple as possible, should expedite progress through good organization, and should be fairly effortless to implement.

Figure 4.1 suggests the division of a meeting into three phases: the *set-up*, the *body*, and the *closure*. At a high level these provide a basic structure that lends itself to most meeting situations. The case studies that follow in Part II will demonstrate how attention to detail within each section can benefit the outcome of the meeting, but first we will introduce the purpose of each.

The set-up

The set-up phase of the meeting generally consists of two activities: *participant introductions* and *setting the context* for the meeting.

Participant introductions

The nominated chairperson within the consulting team will usually open the dialogue, extending courtesies. If the client has not met members of the team before, concise introductions will be needed. Give good consideration to the guidelines provided in Chapter 3, *Establishing Credibility*, as you are presenting

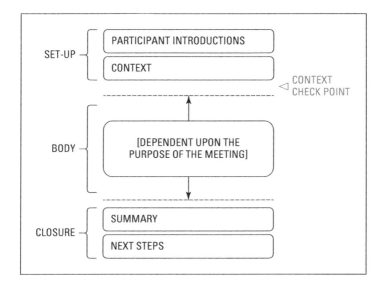

Figure 4.1: Client meeting structure

your proposition and capabilities as a team and will be evaluated accordingly. In some cases it may be appropriate to ask client participants to make brief introductions if there are new faces at the table. When executive-level client representatives are present, however, it may be expected that the consultants have been briefed on their roles in advance.

Agreeing the context

The next step will be to agree the context (or purpose) of the meeting and to ensure that expectations are aligned on both sides. Even if communicated in advance, it is usually worthwhile to reiterate the context at the beginning of the meeting. Closely coupled with the meeting objectives, the context is typically conveyed using a simple phrase such as 'What we would like to do in the meeting today is…'. An example is provided below.

'We have reviewed the requirements that you provided to our colleagues last week. What we would like to do in the meeting today is to share with you some of our solution

ideas, obtain your feedback and to ask you a few additional
questions. Would that be OK?'

As the example suggests, a check point should also be taken:
'Would that be OK?' Unless the *context check point* is taken, the
context has not been agreed. This check point is important for
two reasons:

- As a matter of courtesy. The meeting is taking up not only the
  consultants' time but also the client's time.
- More tactically, to ensure that expectations are aligned. In the
  majority of cases clients may respond 'Yes, that's fine', but if
  any different expectations, needs or priorities exist then these
  will be brought to the surface. The client might respond 'That
  sounds fine. We are particularly interested to hear about solutions related to product development'. The client has just
  shared a new and perhaps important expectation that may
  need to be considered carefully in the way that you direct the
  continued discussion. In the absence of the check point, you
  may have found yourself in the painful situation where after
  presenting material for the first half of the meeting and receiving limited interest, the client eventually says 'I hoped that we
  would discuss product development initiatives … When will
  we get to that?'

A note on check points

Consulting is a dynamic and highly collaborative business. As
consultants, we generally put in good preparation based upon
our own ideas and beliefs, but these will need to be reconciled
with the client's inputs, needs, knowledge of their own organization and ways of working. The use of check points is an excellent way for us to achieve this and incorporates flexibility into
our approach. Based upon the feedback collected at each check
point, we decide how to proceed. Should we continue on our
planned path, or modify our approach? We cannot simply meet

the client, execute our discussion plan and hope that at the end of the meeting everyone will be satisfied.

The body

With the set-up phase completed, credibility has been established, expectations are aligned and we are ready to move forward. The body of the meeting is where the work is done, where the majority of information is exchanged, where discussions take place, agreements are reached, and action items allocated. The structure of the body will vary depending upon the purpose of the meeting and may include the collection of client requirements, the definition of problem scope, or the presentation of analyses, solutions and recommendations. The three case studies that follow in Part II will demonstrate, in particular, different ways in which the body of the meeting can be structured.

The closure

The closure of the meeting generally consists of two activities: A clear *summary*, and agreement on *next steps*.

Summary

A summary is an important part of a meeting. Even if you only have a minute available, make a habit of including a brief summary, unless there is pressure to conclude. When recounting the summary, use your notes and pick up on the most important *details* and *points of agreement* that came out of the discussion. The summary is an excellent opportunity for you demonstrate that you are sharp, on the ball, and have understood precisely the inputs provided. This provides a mature client with the confidence that you have understood what is required and are therefore likely to deliver a good result.

All too often the summary provided at the end of a meeting is weak, based upon poorly captured information that it vaguely articulated. Compare the following two examples of summaries given by different consultants at the conclusion of a meeting with a client in the airline industry.

Example 1

Thank you for the meeting today. We will look into cost reduction and the improvement of selected business processes, the intended fleet replacement programme, as well as the outsourcing of maintenance activities.

Example 2

Thank you for the meeting today. We have understood that your management wishes to reduce operating expenses by 10% within the coming year. You would like us to review selected business processes, beginning with sales and administration, with a view to automation. Regarding the fleet, you would be interested in an analysis concerning your intended Boeing 767 replacement programme, with the Boeing 787 and Airbus A330 as options for medium-haul routes. And, finally, we should look into new outsourcing possibilities for maintenance in the Middle East and North America regions.

These two summaries could have been provided at the conclusion of the same meeting where the same information was shared by the client. From the client's perspective, which of the consultants would you perceive to have a more accurate understanding of your needs? Be concise and accurate when summarizing. Ensure that attention is paid to important details, based upon well-recorded notes.

Next steps

The final agreement to be made concerns clear next steps and a concrete plan for moving forward. This should encompass both the consultants' and the client's perspectives, including a recap of any action items that have been assigned.

'What we will do now is to take your feedback and integrate it into our solution proposal, which will be sent to you via email by 9 a.m. on Friday. We will circulate meeting minutes to all participants by the end of the day today. If you could provide, as agreed, a regional breakdown of your sales figures by close of business tomorrow then we will be in a position to consider this in our analysis.'

The client can see that you are clear, organized and have a plan, which in turn inspires confidence. Commitment is secured by both parties on the action list prior to meeting conclusion.

The post-meeting debrief

Upon conclusion of the meeting, a post-meeting debrief is a way to ensure smooth continuation in the consulting process. The debrief should be conducted as early as possible while events are still fresh in everyone's mind. Avoid the common phenomenon where participants return to the office, head for their desks, read emails, and little further is said about the meeting that took place. Attended by the consultants who participated in the meeting as well as other internal stakeholders who have an interest, the debrief has two main objectives:

- To review the meeting outcomes, determine the approach moving forward and assign internal follow-up tasks such as the completion of agreed action items.
- As a mechanism for continuous learning and development within the consulting team. Discuss in particular:
  - The meeting objectives and how well they were achieved
  - Key lessons based upon client feedback and ways that they should be incorporated into the consulting approach
  - Any difficulties that arose and how they should be handled in the future
  - Feedback to team members regarding both positive performance and areas for improvement.

CHAPTER SUMMARY

The preparation for and execution of a meeting should be considered as a tactical exercise in order to achieve positive outcomes efficiently.

Key preparation activities include:

- The definition of clear meeting objectives that describe what is to be achieved in order for the session to be considered a success
- The composition of a team, of appropriate size, whose participation will be required to meet the objectives
- The formulation of a team plan that includes the clear definition of roles and an approach for handling questions.

Three phases can be used to structure a meeting at the high level:

- A *set-up* phase, comprising credible introductions, a clearly articulated *context* for the discussion, and a *context check point* to ensure that expectations are aligned on both sides
- The *meeting body*, structured with the purpose and objectives of the meeting in mind
- A *closure* phase, comprising a clear and accurate summary and proposed next steps.

A *post-meeting debrief* can be used to maximize the learning from a session through the sharing of individual observations, enabling feedback to be provided to team members as well as the identification of lessons learned for consideration in future engagements.

PART II

CASE STUDIES

This part of the book will demonstrate how the funda-mental principles introduced in Part I can be applied successfully in practice. Three case studies are presented that reflect common consulting situations, each requiring a somewhat different approach.

Case Study 1, set in the consumer electronics industry, exam-ines a meeting whose purpose is to explore a new consulting opportunity and gather initial requirements.

Case Study 2, set in the insurance industry, examines a meeting where consultants are required to discuss a solution approach with a client.

Case Study 3, set in the airline business, examines a meet-ing whose purpose is to engage with a client to agree upon the scope of an analytical study to investigate a complex, yet abstract issue.

The case studies are documented in some detail with the inten-tion that the reader, after reviewing each case, will gain an understanding of how to handle each of these situations.

EXPLORING A NEW CONSULTING OPPORTUNITY

CASE SCENARIO

A manufacturing company in the consumer electronics industry is seeking to achieve improved efficiencies and to lower costs by rationalizing the information technology (IT) systems used to support its business and by optimizing related work processes. At the same time it will be important to ensure that sufficient capacity is available to support future expansion plans. The main systems and processes under consideration relate to the management of component inventories, the planning of production schedules and human resources administration.

Meridian Consulting is one of three companies invited to tender for the assignment, based upon its reputation in both the IT and manufacturing industries. An initial meeting has been set up to discuss the potential opportunity with the chief information officer (CIO) of the client organization.

Dean Farrell is a senior consultant at Meridian and has been assigned to handle the new opportunity. Earlier in the week some background information was conveyed to him by the CIO during a short telephone conversation. The dialogue was informative, although somewhat high level. Dean is used to this as many new consulting opportunities begin this way, making the initial meeting with the client particularly important to establish a more tangible basis for moving forward.

MEETING PREPARATION

Meeting objectives

Dean defines the following objectives for the planned meeting with the CIO.

> - Make a credible impression as a suitable partner
> - Capture the client's requirements more precisely
> - Identify additional stakeholders to be engaged

As other consultancies are under consideration for this assignment, it will be particularly important for Meridian to make a credible impression, positioning itself as a suitable and well-qualified partner to take on the assignment.

During the initial meeting the team will need to capture the client's requirements as accurately as possible.

Finally, as different areas of the business are likely to be impacted, the team should identify any other stakeholders within the client organization who should be involved so that they can be engaged as early as possible. This will reduce the risk of new requirements being introduced late in the process, resulting in unnecessary iterations in their consulting approach.

Composing the team

Having defined the meeting objectives, Dean assembles a team to meet with the client. He plans to bring along two colleagues: Allan Cooper, an IT architect with specific expertise in the domain of manufacturing, and Jeanette Koh, a project manager with substantial experience in the execution of multi-discipline projects.

In a brief internal meeting the three consultants discuss the background provided by the client as well as some pre-meeting preparation that Allan has done.

At the *basic preparation* level, Allan briefs the team on the client's organization and shares the names of three key executives who are likely to have an interest in the project. An overview of the client's product portfolio is presented, comprising four distinct product lines. An analyst report ranked the client fifth in its industry last year.

Detailed preparation has revealed that the client positions itself to offer simplicity, reliability and value for money in its product offerings. Sales are achieved through a network of 100 distributors and are targeted mainly towards domestic consumers and small to medium-sized enterprises. Current industry trends indicate an increase in competition and a shift in consumer preferences towards high-tech products with many features. These factors may have influenced the client's revenue, which has dropped by 6.5% year-on-year and narrowed the focus on improving internal efficiencies. Also noted from the annual report is an increase in receivables, suggesting poor collections performance. In a recent press release the client announced that it would revamp its product portfolio within the coming year to include new feature-rich offerings.

From an *engagement-specific* preparation perspective, Dean briefs the other team members on the information exchanged during the telephone conversation with the CIO. The CIO has promised to share more detailed requirements collected from various departments in his organization during the meeting. With a broad potential assignment scope, the team members agree that capturing clear priorities at an early stage will be important. They brainstorm and make a list of questions that they should ask to enable them to pursue the opportunity accurately. Jeanette takes an action item to identify reference cases related to the areas of inventory management, production planning and human resource administration that are documented in Meridian's internal knowledge-sharing database.

The team plan

The team members decide that they will not bring any presentation slides to the meeting. This is quite common in an initial meeting situation. As the client's needs are not well understood any presentation material would be generic. Instead they plan to craft the dialogue as an across-the-table discussion.

They agree that Dean will take the lead in directing the discussion and the other team members will contribute with their views as appropriate and support the handling of questions. Allan will be the chief note-taker on this occasion and will be responsible for the summary at the meeting's conclusion.

With only a small amount of effort invested and a short internal meeting, the team feels well prepared and ready to engage.

EXPLORING AN OPPORTUNITY: THE SET-UP PHASE

The consulting team arrives at the client's office the next morning and is received by the CIO. After exchanging pleasantries, they begin their discussion. Dean takes the lead and introduces his team.

Participant introductions

Dean: *Thank you for receiving us this morning. Before we start the meeting, I would like to take a moment to introduce the team that I have brought along today.*

This is Allan Cooper. Allan is a senior solution architect with 11 years of experience in the domain of automation solutions, focused mainly on production management and associated processes.

Jeanette Koh has worked as a project manager for 10 years. We asked her to participate today as she has recently completed a similar IT transformation project for a leading semiconductor manufacturer in Germany.

As an organization, Meridian brings substantial experience working with IT support systems and business processes in the manufacturing industry. Should you have any questions regarding our background, we would be happy to address them.

Setting the context

Dean continues, proposing the context for the meeting.

Dean: *What we would like to do in the meeting today is to understand and discuss your requirements at a more detailed level. This will then enable us to identify an optimal solution approach for you. Would that be OK?*

The CIO agrees, making an additional comment: 'I would also be very interested to hear your position regarding data migration approaches for transferring the information in our existing systems to the replacement ones.'

The *context check point* has just revealed a specific client expectation. The consultants make a note of this. If they are able to address this point well during the meeting the expectation will be satisfied. If not, this item should certainly be considered as a follow-up action.

EXPLORING AN OPPORTUNITY: THE MEETING BODY

Directing a discussion to explore a new consulting opportunity requires a disciplined yet flexible approach. This is for two main reasons:

- Early in the consulting process we are often working with thin or limited information. You may have been informed that a client 'is interested in support with cost reduction' or 'is seeking advice regarding marketing strategies'. These are broad statements that could have many implications, and as a result the discussion could unfold in any of several different directions. As consultants, we should be sufficiently prepared to handle any one of these directions, at least at the basic level.
- We may be meeting new client executives for the first time. Clients vary significantly in terms of style and

expectations, and we will need sufficient flexibility to accommodate this, demonstrating the ability to build relationships with a wide variety of individuals, as illustrated by the example below.

A consulting team conducted initial meetings with two different organizations both operating in the pharmaceuticals industry in Belgium. The client executive in the first meeting demonstrated a relaxed and somewhat informal approach to the discussion, sharing his ideas verbosely but providing for the most part good and relevant information. Occasional deviation from planned discussion items meant that the meeting ran for a longer time than expected; however, a good rapport was achieved between the consultants and the client.

The client executive in the second meeting was professional, polite but very straightforward in her approach and seemed keen to put the consultants to the test. She opened the meeting with two questions: 'Could you outline your firm's qualifications for an assignment like this? What differentiates you from other consulting firms that I might consider?'

As the meeting continued, little information was volunteered by the client who was clearly evaluating the way that the consultants would approach the issue. A productive dialogue relied heavily on the consultants' abilities to direct the discussion and pose pertinent questions.

Both meetings yielded successful outcomes; however, the consultants were required to adapt their style quite significantly in order to build relationships with, and meet the expectations of, each client stakeholder.

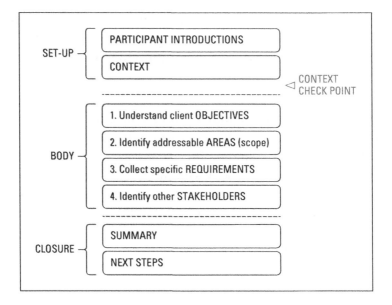

Figure C-1.1: Exploring a new consulting opportunity

Figure C1.1 depicts the structure that the Meridian team members have prepared for the body of their meeting with the CIO. A systematic approach, based around four discussion points, will be required to explore the opportunity with both accuracy and completeness.

Business objectives

The team will first seek to understand the client's *business objectives* for the assignment and how these relate to the organization's strategy as a whole. Client stakeholders often jump straight to their requirements, but prior to this an understanding of the underlying business objectives is required to ensure that the requirements are interpreted in the correct context. A client may say, for example:

'*We have contacted you because we need a new warehouse management system. The system should support the automated scanning of inbound and outbound goods and provide flexible reporting capabilities.'*

An appropriate response from a consultant would be:

'We would be pleased to discuss this with you, but, first of all, what business objectives does your management aim to achieve by changing the warehouse management system? Are you aiming to reduce costs by implementing the solution, or to achieve higher bandwidth through reduced cycle times? What targets have you defined, and how do these relate to the overall strategy of the business?'

Later, when presenting a proposal, this information will be needed by the consultants when explaining how their proposed approach will positively contribute to the client's business. Business objectives must therefore be clearly understood.

Areas to address (scope)

With the objectives understood, the team will move on to discuss the intended *scope* of the assignment. Which areas of the business will need to be addressed in order to achieve the stated business objectives? They plan to ask for the client's view of this first and then complement this with suggestions, based upon Meridian's experience. The practice of *asking before commenting* is an effective way to ensure that both client and consultant knowledge is correctly leveraged and that the scope is correctly tailored to the client's needs. It is also a good way to avoid the perception that the consultants are trying to enforce their own ideas without consideration of the client's unique situation.

The scope of any significant transformation usually requires consideration of three factors: Systems, processes and people. Some clients may focus on only the systems dimension;

however, few business problems are solved purely through the implementation of IT systems. The team is aware that this may need to be raised, once again relative to the agreed business objectives.

Requirements

With agreement on the high-level scope, the nature of the potential assignment will now be emerging. The team will discuss each area to be addressed and collect the client's requirements in each case. Requirements can be quite diverse and may relate to new functions needed within IT systems, the performance targets of processes, human capabilities, and so forth.

Other stakeholders

Finally, consideration needs to be given to other stakeholders within the client organization. When consulting towards larger organizations, multiple departments may be affected by an assignment and corresponding stakeholders will need to be engaged, their cooperation secured and their views understood. An engagement plan will be needed to collect the right requirements from the right people in order to formulate a solution that will correctly address the needs of the organization as a whole.

The proposed approach built around these four points embodies an important logic to ensure both accuracy and completeness:

- If we have not understood a client's business objectives we are unlikely to define, with accuracy, a suitable scope to meet those objectives.
- If the scope has not been correctly defined we will fail to collect the right requirements in the right business areas. Furthermore, it will be difficult to assess which additional stakeholders, if any, should be involved.

EXPLORING AN OPPORTUNITY: THE CLIENT DIALOGUE

Dean initiates the body of the meeting with an open question, encouraging the client to share his thoughts freely and set the scene.

Dean: *We understand that you are planning a type of IT transformation. How can Meridian be of assistance?*

The CIO outlines the background of the intended assignment.

CIO: *We are facing high competition as well as price pressure in our industry. We will soon introduce new and more complex products into our portfolio. This will require some of our most important IT support systems to be either upgraded or replaced. In addition, our CEO is looking to all departments to seek ways to improve internal efficiency.*

This statement, whilst providing a valid starting point, is still somewhat ambiguous. The consultants will need a much more tangible understanding of the client's needs to provide an effective solution. They begin their intended process of exploration.

Objectives

Dean: *We understand. Indeed, many corporations are able to harness new capabilities and improve efficiencies through the targeted deployment of IT. Given the current strategy of your company, how would you define the specific business objectives for this assignment?*

The client pauses thoughtfully for a second, not having framed his organization's needs in the form of specific business objectives.

CIO: *The successful introduction of our new product portfolio will be instrumental to our CEO's vision to grow our sales. Here in the IT department our primary objective is to upgrade critical IT systems as required to support its introduction, ensuring that needed functionalities and sufficient capacity are in place. This is my primary responsibility. Finally, we will need to identify opportunities to lower our operational costs.*

The consultants note these objectives. They ask a final question to quantify the stated objectives.

Dean: *Do you have any timelines in mind, or targets in terms of increased sales, capacity improvements or operational costs savings?*

CIO: *Yes. We would like any new IT platforms to be deployed within one year to align with our new product launch plan. I am unable to share specific sales targets, but our company has the ambition to increase sales by 50% in the next three years. And regarding improved efficiencies, I would be keen to hear your experience as to the types of gains that can generally be realized from an assignment like this.*

The consultants respond, sharing some indicative examples from other projects based upon Jeanette's research during preparation. Further analysis will, however, be required to establish the gains that would be realistic within this client's business.

By asking a few simple questions the client's initial statement of need has been translated into three specific objectives, refined through discussion, and quantified where possible. The value

OBJECTIVE	TARGET	TIME
Grow sales	50%	3 years
Upgrade or replace IT systems as required for new portfolio	•	1 year
Reduce operational costs	TBD	TBD

TBD = To be determined

Figure C-1.2: Collected business objectives

that the client organization seeks to derive by conducting the assignment is becoming clearer.

The consultants briefly summarize the business objectives that have been agreed (see Figure C-1.2). This is only an initial statement of objectives that is likely to be further refined during further discussions as the opportunity unfolds.

Scope

With an initial understanding of the business objectives, the consultants proceed to the next point in their approach.

Dean: *Which IT systems do you feel will need to be considered in order to meet these business objectives?*

CIO: *I have had dialogues with the various heads of departments to establish their areas of need. It has become clear that we will need to replace our component inventory management system. The current system will not be able to support the increased number of components required by our new products. We will also need to address the area of production planning and put in place new functionalities to handle more complex production schedules. And our head of human resources is requesting better support systems to*

> *eliminate a number of manual administration processes.*

Dean: *How would you prioritize these areas?*

CIO: *The inventory management system is our top priority. It is a system that is already under stress and should have been replaced some time ago. The production planning system would rank second, and the human resources system third.*

The CIO has suggested three areas to be included in the scope. Having noted his position, the consultants make additional suggestions based upon their experience and the preparation done prior to the meeting.

Dean: *We note from your annual report that receivables have been increasing over the last three years disproportionately to sales. Is this a concern for your management, and should the financial collections systems and processes be considered within this assignment?*

The client responds, impressed by the diligence of the consultants.

CIO: *This is a valid comment, and indeed a point of concern for our management. If you have any solutions that you would like to propose in this area we would be open to consider them.*

Allan makes another enquiry.

Allan: *We understand that you plan to introduce new and somewhat more complex products in your portfolio offering. Do you feel that this will* *require any investments in the area of customer relationship management (CRM)?*

The client responds, referring to an internal discussion.

CIO: *I had also envisioned that we might need to act in the area of CRM; however, our head of marketing feels that we have sufficient capabilities for the short term. He would like to address this area next year when we plan some major changes to our sales channels.*

Recognizing that successful transformation within an organization is rarely achieved by the implementation of IT systems alone, Dean raises the process- and people-related dimensions.

Dean: *To transform successfully and to achieve the objectives that you have stated, a number of other aspects beyond systems will usually need to be considered. You may need to adapt your working processes and to leverage the functionalities offered by new systems. New competences may be required, and there may be opportunities to improve efficiencies through process optimization or by simplifying your organization. Are these aspects that you would like us to consider as part of this assignment?*

The CIO is open to this suggestion.

CIO: *My team tends to focus on the systems implementation aspect, but you are quite correct, failure to consider processes and staff competence may delay realization of the business benefits from these new solutions. I would be open to receive your proposals in this area.*

IN SCOPE		
1. Inventory management		
– IT capabilities	Required	
– Process & organization	Open for discussion	
– People competence	Open for discussion	
1. Production planning		
– IT capabilities	Required	
– Process & organization	Open for discussion	
– People competence	Open for discussion	
1. Human resources administration		
– IT capabilities	Required	
– Process & organization	Open for discussion	
– People competence	Open for discussion	
2. Financial collections		
– IT capabilities	Open for discussion	
– Process & organization	Open for discussion	
– People competence	Open for discussion	
OUT OF SCOPE:		
Customer relationship management		

Figure C-1.3: Initial scope

The consulting team is pleased to hear this reaction, knowing that a solution able to drive the desired business outcomes will require the consideration of these additional aspects. By listening to the client's view and then contributing with their recommendations an initial agreement has been made on a scope for the assignment (Figure C-1.3).

Requirements

The consultants continue to discuss the client's requirements in each area that has been identified within the potential scope. The types of questions that they ask could be categorized as follows:

As-is analysis Within each area under consideration, how do things work today? Aspects discussed include current processes and working procedures, the structure of responsible organizations, existing systems in use and associated workflows.

Pain points Are there identified pain points that should be addressed in their solution approach? What things do not work well or may not work well in the future? Pain points can relate to error rates, costs of operation, poor response time, poor customer satisfaction, and so forth.

New functionalities required What new functionalities are required in business processes or IT systems? These typically relate to the new capabilities that an organization wishes to deploy.

Other non-functional requirements Non-functional requirements may relate to considerations such as performance, quality or innovation.

The CIO provides an overview of the processes and systems that are currently in use for component inventory management. The existing system is not user-friendly and requires incoming stock to be logged manually. The component ordering procedure is often carried out inaccurately, resulting in stock levels of up to 20% in excess of what is required. The replacement system should support the reporting of delivery statistics on an hourly basis and manage component build lists for at least

100 product configurations. Automation should allow the size of the team managing the warehouse to be reduced, delivering an associated reduction in cost. Finally, it is agreed that new competences should be developed to improve the performance of operations and to minimize error rates.

Similar requirements are recorded for each in-scope area. Allan takes the opportunity to explain Meridian's approach for defining a data migration strategy, referring to lessons learned from previous projects. The client is pleased to hear this account as it relates to a particular point of concern.

Stakeholders

As the proposed assignment will impact several departments within the client organization, the team enquires about other stakeholders who should be involved.

Jeanette: *Are there any other stakeholders whom we should consult in your organization who may have requirements to contribute?*

CIO: *Yes. You should definitely meet with our chief operations officer. Both component inventory management and production planning are processes that are managed by his organization. It may also be advisable for you to talk to our head of marketing who can elaborate on the details of our new product portfolio, and our head of human resources in order to hear her requirements first hand.*

Anticipating the discussions that will take place with these individuals, Jeanette asks the CIO proactively about their views.

Jeanette: *We would be pleased to meet with them. How do they feel about the proposed changes? Have they expressed any particular views or concerns?*

CIO: *Operations will be very keen to discuss the component inventory management. They are having a lot of problems in this area. Marketing, on the other hand, will be focused on timelines. They want to launch the new products as quickly as possible. Human resources is keen to look for new tools to play a more strategic role in our organization.*

The consultants nod, knowing that this information will be helpful in preparing for their subsequent meetings with operations, marketing and human resources. When meeting these stakeholders they will not need to start with a blank sheet of paper, but rather can use the insights provided by the CIO to anticipate needs, questions and concerns.

EXPLORING AN OPPORTUNITY: THE CLOSURE PHASE

Summary

Allan refers to his notes and provides a concise summary.

"Thank you for the meeting today. We have understood that your organization aims to implement IT systems and process improvements within a year in order to support the introduction of a new product portfolio. New processes are expected to deliver improved efficiencies and should have sufficient capacity to support a growth in sales of up to 50% during the next three years.

The areas of the business that you would like us to focus on are component inventory management, production planning, human resources administration and financial collections.

In the area of inventory management a new solution should support automated logging of incoming stock, enable improved accuracy in order processing, and manage build lists for up to 100 product configurations…'

Allan continues to summarize the requirements collected in each area.

Next steps

Allan continues:

'We would be pleased to meet with your chief operations officer and your heads of marketing and human resources to understand their detailed requirements.

What we will do now is to take the information that you have provided, arrange these meetings and begin work on our solution analysis. We would recommend a brief meeting in one week to update you on our progress and may contact you with additional questions in the meantime.'

The client acknowledges the summary, thanks the consultants for attending and the meeting concludes.

THE MEETING OUTCOME

The consultants return to their office and conduct a debriefing session. They are satisfied with the outcome of the meeting and feel that their meeting objectives were achieved. A particular asset was their success in framing the opportunity by identifying the client's business objectives, initial scope and requirements in a single meeting by crafting their dialogue systematically. Dean takes an action item to make contact with the three other client executives to schedule appointments. Jeanette and Allan agree to carry out preparations for these meetings.

The client also reflects on his meeting with Meridian. They seem to have a strong and experienced team, something that will be crucial for this important assignment. The team had clearly taken the trouble to develop an understanding of his organization in advance, recorded the information provided with accuracy and answered his questions well. He has agreed to meet with two other consulting firms who are potential candidates for this assignment and wonders how the experiences of engaging with them will compare.

CHAPTER SUMMARY

Using a case study, this chapter has illustrated how some of the concepts introduced in Part I can be applied in practice. As in a real-life consulting situation:

- Preparation was performed and contributed to both efficient progress during the meeting and positive client perceptions.
- The agreement of meeting objectives and a team plan enabled the consultants to work professionally and effectively to achieve their goal.
- The meeting was organized into three phases: The set-up phase, the meeting body and the closure.
- During the set-up phase a check point taken at the context revealed an additional client expectation, providing a valuable input to the consultants. They were able to satisfy this expectation later during the progress of the meeting.
- The body of the meeting was structured according to its purpose: To explore a new consulting opportunity. This was achieved efficiently through the use of a systematic approach built around four discussion points:
  - Capture of business objectives
  - Agreement on the required assignment scope
  - Collection of requirements
  - Identification of additional stakeholders.
- During the discussion the 'ask-then-comment' technique was used to understand the client's initial position before attempting to influence or recommend. Understanding a client's initial thinking is important and provides the foundation for a discussion where agreement can be reached efficiently.

PRESENTING A SOLUTION APPROACH

CASE SCENARIO

Dasser Consulting has been engaged by a medium-sized insurance company in the UK that is under pressure to reshape its business. Focused purely on life and health insurance offerings, the company has done well over the recent decade, due partly to a strong product offering but also to a prospering economy. But now that a recession is shrinking the size of the addressable market, insurance companies are competing harder for a reduced stream of new business and the client is concerned about its future.

A week ago two senior consultants from Dasser met with the client to gain an understanding of the assignment, establishing the client's business objectives, scope, initial requirements and the stakeholders who should be engaged in subsequent discussions. Since then they have carried out basic solution analysis specific to the client's situation and have considered possible approaches and their benefits.

They have now scheduled a meeting to discuss their proposed solution approach with the director of operations in the client organization.

MEETING PREPARATION

Meeting objectives

The Dasser team has defined the following objectives for their meeting.

- Make a credible impression as a suitable partner
- Test and validate initial solution proposals
- Collect additional information required to refine the solution approach at the detailed level

Although Dasser has already been selected for this assignment, the team members will ensure that they make a credible impression, an objective that is generally associated with any client meeting. This constitutes an important part of the relationship-building process for the project that will follow. In addition, two attending team members have not met the client executive before, and the credibility that they build will influence the way in which their contributions are received.

An important objective for the meeting will be to present and validate their initial solution proposals. Each proposal has been drafted based upon the consultants' understanding of the client's business and objectives, coupled with their experience from previous consulting projects. The client's validation of each proposal, however, will be critical. Will the solution ideas be feasible within the target organization? And what success factors or obstacles will need to be considered?

Finally, additional information will be needed to further develop each solution proposal that is to be pursued.

Composing the team

One of the senior consultants who attended the initial meeting, Sue Jarvis, will lead the discussion. She will be accompanied by two other consultants, Daniel Ross, a consultant with six years of experience in the area of organizational development, and Sean Adler, who brings five years of experience working with automation solutions in the financial services and insurance industries. The two consultants have been closely involved in the solution analysis activities since the initial meeting and have formulated the recommendations that are to be presented.

The pre-meeting preparation that was prepared prior to the initial engagement was documented and shared with the two new team members. They had familiarized themselves with the client situation and reviewed the minutes from the initial meeting before starting work on their solution proposals.

The team plan

Sue will act as the chairperson on behalf of the consulting team. The various solution proposals will be presented by Daniel and Sean, who will handle questions within their areas of expertise, supported by Sue as needed. Sue has decided to take the lead in note-taking on this occasion, allowing the consultants to focus on their contributions and the associated discussions.

PRESENTING A SOLUTION APPROACH:
THE SET-UP PHASE

On the day of the meeting the consultants arrive punctually at the client's office. They are greeted warmly by the director. Sue introduces the two new team members and proceeds to set the context.

Sue: *We have reviewed the information that you provided last week and have carried out some initial solution analysis. What we would like to do in the meeting today is to share some of our solution ideas, obtain your feedback and ask a few additional questions. Would that be OK?*

Client: *That's fine. Following our management meeting this morning, I would be particularly interested to hear about any solutions that you have prepared related to cost control.*

Again an important expectation has been captured at the context check point. During consulting engagements clients' priorities may change, hence the importance of taking these check points. Having prepared solutions options targeting both revenue development and cost control, the consultants understand immediately that they may need to adapt the focus of their presentation towards the reduction of costs.

PRESENTING A SOLUTION APPROACH:
THE MEETING BODY

The consultants have structured the body of their meeting around two main discussion points and have prepared a set of presentation slides to support the dialogue (Figure C-2.1).

First, they plan a brief review of the business objectives that were agreed in the first meeting. This will enable them to capture any changes in direction or priorities that may have

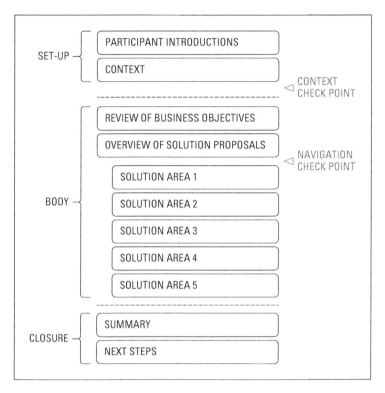

Figure C-2.1: Presenting a solution approach

occurred. Irrespective of such changes, it is advisable to spend a few minutes reminding participants of the agreed business objectives before presenting solution proposals, to ensure that the proposals are evaluated in the correct context. All too often consultants present solutions without reference to the underlying business objectives. Their presentations may be delivered well but leave the client thinking: 'That was an interesting presentation, but would the solutions presented really solve my problem?' In consulting, the linkage between business objectives and solutions is critical at every point.

Having done this, they will move swiftly to the main focus of the meeting and present the solutions proposals that they have prepared. Having considered the client's objectives holistically, they have defined solutions in five areas that they plan to put forward. As the duration of the meeting is only one hour, the skill of time and content management will therefore be important.

PRESENTING A SOLUTION APPROACH: THE CLIENT DIALOGUE

Sue continues, referring to the first slide in their presentation (Figure C-2.2).

Sue: *Further to the discussion last week, our understanding of your business objectives for this assignment is to reduce costs and deploy initiatives to increase sales. You indicated that operational costs should be reduced by 10% within the year, as well as an ambition to increase revenue from sales by 10% in the same time period. Are you in agreement with these objectives?*

The head of operations responds.

Client: *Yes. However, following a management meeting this morning, the pressure on cost reduction has increased. Our management now expects a reduction in operational costs of closer to 20%.*

REVIEW OF BUSINESS OBJECTIVES		
OBJECTIVE	**TARGET**	**TIME FRAME**
Increase sales	10%	1 year
Reduce operational costs	10%	1 year
		Dasser

Figure C-2.2: Review of business objectives

```
SOLUTION AREAS

Development of new products
Streamlining of sales organization
Automation of administrative processes
Recruitment and training of sales staff
Introduction of new sales channels
                                        Dasser
```

Figure C-2.3: Candidate solution areas

The consultants make a note of this feedback and continue to their next presentation slide (Figure C-2.3).

Sue: *Based upon our analysis, we have identified five candidate areas in which we believe that we could help you progress towards achieving your objectives. We have prepared some material in each area which my colleagues will present.*

First, you might consider the development of new products to provide clearer differentiation from competitors. Second, we have identified opportunities to streamline your existing sales organization and achieve the same reach that you have today but with lower cost. The automation of certain administrative processes could also deliver significant savings. We have considered how the recruitment and training of staff could result in a more targeted and effective sales approach. And finally, we have considered new sales channels such as partnerships with other financial institutions.

At this point the consultants take an important *navigation check point* that will affect the flow of the discussion that follows.

Sue: *Before we discuss these areas in detail, we would like to ask for your initial feedback. Do you agree that these areas are relevant? Do you feel that any area has been missed? And if not, which of the areas would be of greatest interest to you?*

The client pauses momentarily and then responds.

Client : *A new product development initiative is already under way. We did not raise this with you earlier as we have kept our plans somewhat confidential. We have carried out extensive market research and competitor analysis and intend to bring a new updated product offering to the market within three months.*

The streamlining of our sales organization is certainly of interest, as is the automation of processes. We have deployed some initiatives in these areas ourselves but with limited success. We need support with these activities.

Recruitment and training could be discussed; however, we feel that the number of sales people that we have is sufficient. Any recruitment would need to be limited to specific areas where we lack specialist competence such as corporate sales. This, however, is not a high priority.

We have considered partnerships with banks in the past, but this was not approved at our top management level. The reasons are somewhat political, but overall the approach was considered to carry too high a risk. It would not be appropriate to raise it again at this time.

The consultants respond to this feedback.

Sue: *Thank you. Based upon what you have said, we will omit the discussion on product development unless you are interested in additional inputs. We can start our discussion today with the topics of streamlining and automation. We will not discuss partnerships as this is clearly out of scope, and if time permits we can discuss recruitment as this is currently a lower priority for you. Would this approach be OK?*

The client agrees and a productive discussion of each topic follows, based upon the material that has been prepared, led by Daniel and Sean.

A note on navigation

The use of presentation slides to support the discussion of solution approaches can be very powerful in consulting. At the same time there is a danger of bringing a 20-slide presentation to a client and simply executing it from beginning to end, whether the client finds it relevant or not. Some consultants have a reputation for this. We worked for hours designing these slides, they think, so we must present them.

A good consulting approach requires an element of *flexibility*. We can formulate strategies, leverage industry best practices and prepare solutions based upon our experience, but ultimately these are targeted towards a client's business and no one understands the client's business better than the client.

As illustrated in this case study, it is therefore advisable to introduce each approach briefly and then take a check point, which we will refer to as a *navigation check point*. Some options may be eliminated immediately and will not need to be discussed at all, and the relative importance of other topics can be established. All you are doing is navigating efficiently to the most relevant areas by leveraging the client's knowledge of his or her organization.

Good navigation is an important skill when delivering presentations to clients. The amount of navigation possible varies according to the material to be presented and, in particular, the dependencies between different topics. In the end you may not use all of your presentation slides or use them in the order that you had initially intended, but you are likely to address your clients' needs more accurately and therefore receive higher appreciation.

Do not feel constrained because the topics in your presentation are already sequenced in a particular order. Most clients will not mind if you flick past a few slides to reach a particular topic and are more likely to be impressed that you are addressing their needs appropriately. Furthermore, many of today's presentation tools provide the option to alter the order of the presented slides in real time.

By navigating to the most relevant issues early in the meeting you will also optimize the use of time. If time runs short the most important topics will be have been discussed and it will be the least important topics that are postponed.

Consulting is a dynamic business:
Good Preparation + Flexibility = Consulting Performance

THE MEETING OUTCOME

During the meeting each of the relevant candidate solution areas was addressed at some length. With regard to the organization, it was agreed that the number of sales offices could be reduced if certain tasks could be centralized. The client committed to providing additional cost and sales information pertaining to each office to enable further analysis on this point.

The consultants made suggestions, based upon their experience, regarding processes that it could be advantageous to automate. It was agreed that automation should be focused on sales support processes initially and an approach was outlined. The client decided to structure the assignment into two phases and to postpone recruitment and training activities until phase two.

After the meeting the consultants held a debrief at their office and reviewed their meeting objectives. They felt that they were able to make a credible impression and demonstrate a well-organized and sufficiently flexible approach to arrive at a suitable solution approach quickly. Good feedback and additional information were collected for each of the solution areas prioritized by the client.

The client had commended the consultants at the end of the meeting, impressed by the breadth of their approach, yet with an ability to adapt and arrive quickly at a solution approach suited to the needs of his organization. 'Some of the consultants we have worked with bring in very lengthy presentations ...', he commented.

THE ROLE OF AN ADVISER: CHALLENGING YOUR CLIENT

The case study presented in this chapter described a situation where the consultants and the client were able to reach agreement quite easily on the solution areas that should be prioritized. This may not always be the case.

Consider a situation where a client dismisses a solution approach that based upon the consultants' experience, could be crucial. Should the consultants accept this view and abandon the idea? Provided that you have established sufficient credibility, it is normally acceptable to contest your client's opinion, and this is a key part of your role as an adviser. Provided that you adopt a constructive and diplomatic approach, clients will usually respect you for this.

A consulting company in North America working in the automotive industry advised a long-standing client to replace an ageing, yet business-critical support system. The consultants suggested that this action was wise considering the company's ongoing technology strategy, but would more importantly eliminate the risk of potential capacity shortages in the short to medium term. The client reviewed this advice but elected to decline the recommendation, stating that the existing system would meet their needs for the foreseeable future. The consultants acknowledged this respectfully.

A year later the client ran into serious capacity problems and had to make large financial outlays to remedy the situation. It was only then that they realized that in the first discussion the consultants' recommendation had been correct and their response short-sighted. 'Why did you not push us?' remarked the client in a later discussion with the consultants. 'Why did you not come back to us last year and insist on the importance of taking action?'

As a consultant you are an adviser. An adviser who simply agrees with the client's position every time is of little value. If you think that your client is about to make a mistake then challenge them, constructively, with good arguments and use the credibility that you have built to do so. Keep in mind, however, that this situation can also work in reverse, as illustrated by the example below.

A consulting team was engaged to design a business solution for a client in Scandinavia. The solution approach was formulated in three parts, each designed to address a specific issue recognized within the client organization. Having already conducted a number of successful projects together with the client, a good relationship was already in place.

When the first part of the solution approach was presented it received positive feedback and the clients provided further inputs for use in its refinement. The second part received similar feedback and plans were discussed for its implementation. When the third part of the approach was presented, however, the clients listened in earnest, considered the recommendations but elected not to adopt them. 'We will move forward based upon the first two solution areas', they concluded.

After the meeting the consultants discussed the feedback that had been provided. They were somewhat disappointed by the response to the third part of their approach, having seen it produce excellent results in another organization. They decided to re-engage and raise the matter with the client again. In a subsequent meeting they put their best efforts into presenting the approach and emphasizing its benefits. The clients listened willingly, but at the end of the meeting their position was unchanged. The feedback, in short, was 'that type of approach will not work well here'. The matter was concluded and the assignment moved forward based upon the areas that had been agreed.

During the subsequent months the consultants worked closely with the client, interacting regularly with the parts of their organization affected by the project. As their familiarity with the client's organization increased they realized that the client had been right. The rejected solution approach would probably never have been embraced by the people working there. It was simply not a good fit for their culture and ways of working.

In consulting we are passionate about formulating recommendations and designing solutions to meet our clients' business needs. As emphasized in this chapter, regardless of the expertise and experience we bring to the table, every client situation is unique and nobody understands the client's business better than the client. This makes the process of validating any solution approach and leveraging client knowledge particularly important.

Moreover, one of the principal limitations to the value that we can add is our clients' willingness to act. Be ready to support recommendations with good arguments, seek to understand and address concerns, but remember that ultimately as consultants we are advisers and the client is the business owner and decision-maker.

CHAPTER SUMMARY

Supported by a case study, this chapter has illustrated the following points:

- Consulting is a dynamic business. How well you perform as a consultant is largely due to how good your preparation is and how flexible you are. Use check points to help maintain such flexibility. Do not just deliver your presentation from beginning to end and congratulate yourself on a good job.

- Navigation is a technique that is valuable when presenting solution options to clients. Instead of forcing the client to listen to a long presentation, it enables us to home in quickly on areas of interest and to address them efficiently. Good navigation also leads to a more interesting and engaging presentation.

- Regardless of the expertise and experience consultants bring to the table, no one knows the client's business better than the client. It is important that we can bring these views together to create a tailored solution.

- A good consultant should be a good adviser. Challenging your client's view constructively and respectfully, supported by good argumentation, is part of an adviser's role. There are, however, limitations. Presenting a proposal again and again that has not secured interest may damage the relationship, and cultural factors may need to be considered. A delicate balance is required, and it is important to know when to back down.

SCOPING A STUDY

Analysis constitutes an important part of the work that we do in consulting and enables us to fully understand an issue and associated alternatives before we prescribe a solution. Often packaged into an activity referred to as a *study*, this may involve *situational analysis* conducted to gain a deeper understanding of a client's existing situation, *requirements analysis* to establish a client's specific needs, *competitor analysis* to benchmark competitor performance and examine competitor strategies, and *solution analysis* to explore and evaluate solution options. The upfront efforts invested in analysis can have a notable influence on the accuracy and subsequent value that a solution can deliver.

Clients may, however, be sceptical towards commissioning consultants to conduct analysis and expect us instead to jump directly to the recommendation of a solution. Common reactions include: 'You are experts in this industry. Why is the analysis of external factors required? You should know these things already', or 'You should not need to analyse the specifics of our organization. You have worked with us many times before.' Most seasoned consultants have heard statements like this more than once. These claims, whilst somewhat legitimate, can reduce the analytical efforts required but rarely render them redundant.

Experience suggests that there are two common reasons for such scepticism. The first and most obvious is cost control. By omitting a study, the client will reduce the financial outlay related to the consulting service. Some may believe that this omission will have no significant impact on the solution delivered, or in some cases may assume that the consultancy will conduct a limited study in any case at their own expense.

A second and less obvious reason relates to the nature of the assignment itself. When a client commissions consultants to carry out a study it is, by default, a somewhat open-ended assignment. The client does not know exactly what it will get for its money; the consultants may deliver a report containing impressive information that helps to understand and solve a problem, or alternatively a report containing data and findings that the client does not find useful at all. Most seasoned clients can refer to at least one situation when they commissioned analysis and were somewhat dissatisfied with the delivered output. A senior executive in Italy referred to one such situation, pointing to a report lying on a coffee table in her office.

'I engaged some local consultants to carry out a market study to assist us in our business planning. That is the report that they delivered. It cost us a small fortune. How are we supposed to use this information to support our planning process? It will be a long time before we engage consultants for an assignment like this again.'

If we are to gain support from clients to conduct essential analytical activities, we will need a way to demonstrate the value of the analysis upfront and not just upon completion of the study. Furthermore, we will need to ensure that any analysis we do is scoped accurately to address the client's need, thus ensuring that the output will be recognized as valuable. The case study presented in this chapter will illustrate how this can be achieved through the use of a technique that is commonly used in the consulting industry.

CASE SCENARIO

A senior manager working for a leading passenger airline is concerned about the profitability of the business. The industry as a whole is under pressure, fuel prices are high, and with operations spanning more than 20 countries he needs to make strategic decisions that will deliver short-term profit improvements. Having executed a number of internal initiatives, he has decided to approach external consultants and to evaluate the additional value that they could add. He has elected to engage with Kura Consulting, a firm with experience in a number of industries including the airline business, although not an airline specialist. There are a number of airline-specific consultancies that he could have approached, but he is keen to see how lessons learned from other industries could be leveraged beyond the traditional practices within his industry. The question posed to the consultants, however, is an open-ended one: 'What steps should we take to increase our profit?'

Kura has assigned two consultants to the task. Tony Peterson is a principal consultant with nine years of experience in management consulting, one year of which relates to airline operations. Fran Meyer is a junior analyst who graduated recently from a reputable university and has worked for six months with Kura. They familiarize themselves with the client's business by carrying out routine preparation activities and agree upon their objectives for the meeting.

MEETING PREPARATION

Meeting objectives

The Kura team has defined the following objectives for their meeting.

- Make a credible impression as a consulting team
- Agree on the scope of a study aimed to identify profit improvement opportunities
- Collect additional information related to the proposed areas within the scope

---

Agreement with the client on a suitable scope for the potential study is an important objective for this meeting. There are many factors in a commercial airline company that could be analysed with regard to improved profitability, and an exhaustive study would take months if not years to carry out. A more accurately directed approach will be required to identify the most beneficial areas of focus and to meet the client's expectations for short-term improvements.

One option would be to simply ask the client 'Which areas should our study cover in order to help you improve profitability?' Many clients may not, however, have a clear answer to this question. Furthermore, they are likely to expect guidance on how to approach the issue and may respond with a statement such as 'You tell me. You are the experts!' As in many consulting situations, the team will need to find a way to combine their own experience, guidance and analytical capabilities with the client's knowledge of the business to determine an optimal way forward.

The team plan

Tony and Fran spend an afternoon preparing for their discussion with the client. They plan to use a logic tree, a consulting technique that can be applied in several different ways. During an internal brainstorming session they plan to sketch out an initial tree as a hypothesis, detailing, based upon their knowledge of the domain, potential causes of the issue that would be candidates for analysis. They then plan to present this work to the client as a basis for collecting input and tailoring the approach to accurately target the organization's specific needs.

On a whiteboard the consultants make a note of the issue to be analysed, 'low profit', and then begin to identify potential contributing causes. For an airline company an exhaustive list of causes could be identified, spanning from high fuel costs to insufficient marketing. To ensure completeness in their approach, they employ a structured, top-down approach by first identifying the main groups of potential causes that should be considered and then later breaking them down. In this case *high costs* and *low revenues* are identified as the most appropriate groups to structure a profitability issue and are sketched as the main branches of their tree, as illustrated in Figure C-3.1.

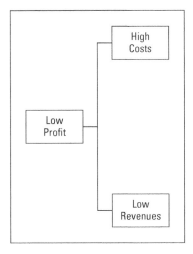

Figure C-3.1: Logic tree: Main branches

The analysis of most issues could be structured in several different ways. Another approach might have been to categorize the potential causes according to *internal factors* and *external factors*, or to group them according to areas of the business where the causes of reduced profit could originate such as *sales*, *marketing* and *operations*. When defining the main branches of a logic tree, whilst there is no 'right answer', it is important to ensure that:

1. The main groups defined cover, to the best of your knowledge, the entire scope of the problem and encompass, collectively, all potential causes.
2. The breakdown is logical and will be easy to follow when later presented to the client.

With the main branches of the tree defined, the team then proceeds to break down these groups systematically, level by level, adding sub-branches as required, and finally the specific causes themselves, which become the leaves of the tree. Their output is illustrated in Figure C-3.2.

Their completed diagram presents a hypothesis listing causes that could potentially contribute to low profit within the client's business, prepared based upon their existing knowledge of the client and the industry domain. As a second step, they plan to refine the tree during the meeting by presenting and validating the hypothesis and leveraging the client's detailed knowledge of his business, homing in on areas of concern and establishing priorities.

It is agreed that Tony will drive the meeting discussion and Fran will capture the client's feedback, identifying areas where further input will be required and summarizing the session. The diagram is printed in poster format so that it can be annotated in real time during the meeting. The next morning the two consultants meet with the client.

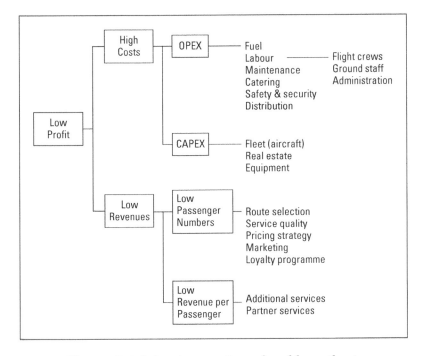

Figure C-3.2: Logic tree: Completed hypothesis

SCOPING A STUDY: THE SET-UP PHASE

After the exchange of courtesies, the consultants make their introductions and set the context for the meeting.

Tony: *My name is Tony Peterson. I have nine years of experience in management consulting, specializing in the area of process optimization within large-scale transportation organizations. One year of my experience comes from the airline business and I have also worked extensively with the haulage industry, which faces many similar challenges.*

Joining me today is Fran Meyer who will be working with me on this assignment. Fran is in her first year at Kura Consulting. We selected her for this assignment due to her strong analytical background, which will be an important asset for the task at hand.

What we would like to do in the meeting today is to present some of the factors, based upon our experience, that are likely to affect the profitability of an organization like yours. We would then like to ask for your feedback so that the approach can be tailored in line with your needs. Perhaps some of the factors can be eliminated if they do not relate to actual areas of concern and we can then agree upon the areas that should be pursued to deliver benefits efficiently. Would that be OK?

The client agrees to the proposed approach.

SCOPING A STUDY: THE CLIENT DIALOGUE

The consultants unfold the tree diagram and the client takes a moment to review it. As the client may not be familiar with the use of the technique, Tony introduces it briefly.

Tony: *This tree diagram represents a simple way for us to break down an issue, in this case 'low profit', and structure a discussion to identify the most critical causes quickly.*

As you can see, we have organized the tree around two main groups: Causes related to high costs, and causes related to low revenues. We would first like to ask if you find this division appropriate, and if you feel that anything else should be considered. Otherwise, which of the groups is of greater priority to you?

A logic tree can expedite the process of identifying critical issues, but it will only do so if appropriate navigation is applied to the discussion. With this in mind a navigation check point has been taken at the branch level to understand the relative priorities of the high-level items before proceeding further. The client responds.

Client: *Both areas are important. Another major area that we are working with is 'regulations'. Although it affects revenue generation possibilities as well as costs, we tend to separate it, and it is a hot topic in the industry today. Most likely we will not look for external assistance, however, in the regulations area just yet.*

Tony takes a pencil and adds an additional branch, 'regulations', to the diagram for completeness. Fran makes a note of the client's feedback. The client continues.

Client: *Regarding priorities, we have spent the last three years running cost optimization initiatives, and whilst I have no doubt that we could make further improvements, we must also grow the top line of our business. I would therefore assign 'low revenues' as the highest priority, 'regulations' in second place, and finally 'high costs'.*

Tony notes the priorities against each branch.

Tony: *Excellent. Let's move on to look at the specific causes that we have anticipated under each area, beginning with low revenues. We have considered both passenger numbers and revenue per passenger, as well as a list of subordinate items in each case. Which of the listed causes are most* *relevant to you, and are there other items that should be considered?*

Client: *From a route selection perspective our company is quite strong. I am satisfied with our long-haul route offering, and also short to medium haul, where we also offer some seasonal routes. Our average passenger yield in these categories is approximately 89%. A challenge remains around domestic routes, some of which are not profitable. This could be an area where further analysis is required.*

Fran asks the client if he would be able to provide a list of domestic routes indicating the average yield and profitability of each. It is agreed that this information will be provided in document form. The client continues.

Client: *Service quality is very important to us, as this is where we aim to outperform our competitors. We put all of our customer-facing staff through a service skills update programme last year and the resulting customer feedback has been positive. This is not an area of concern.*

From a pricing perspective, we are slightly more expensive than competitors in our home market, but offer a strong brand and service level. In other markets we aim to be highly price-competitive. This strategy has worked well.

Marketing is under control and we have made some changes to our public relations approach this year. We are also satisfied with our loyalty programme.

Tony annotates the diagram, highlighting the areas that require investigation and striking out those that appear to be out of scope. He challenges the client regarding the area of marketing.

Tony: *Are you building relationships with your customers through social media and on-line communities?*

Client: *No, we are not. This is a good point. Perhaps there is a gap in our approach and could be something to investigate. It would be interesting to look into what our competitors are doing in this area.*

Marketing remains in scope further to the consultants' suggestion. As the discussion continues, it emerges that further revenue potential could be associated with the introduction of additional value-added services. The client suggests the addition of an item that is not on the tree, *bundled offerings*, related in particular to hotels and ground transfers. Tony adds this.

During a subsequent discussion of the 'high costs' branch, opportunities to reduce labour costs through the simplification of administrative processes are recognized, mainly within regional offices located in South America and South East Asia. It is agreed that there should be further opportunities to optimize the use of real estate, even though some work has already been done in this area. The other items listed are considered to be under control.

The final marked-up logic tree is shown in Figure C-3.3. The consultants ask the client to prioritize the highlighted areas and make a note of his responses on the diagram, and suitable next steps are discussed in each case. Tony asks the client if he has anything further to add and then hands over to Fran to summarize.

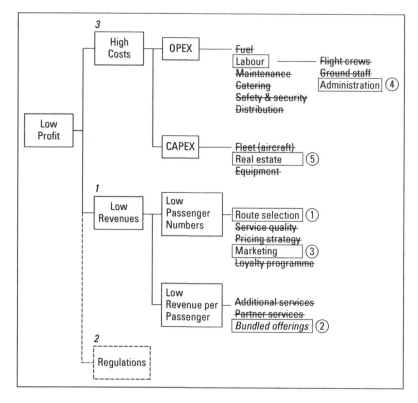

Figure 3.3: The logic tree: with client feedback

Fran: *Thank you for the meeting today. What we have understood is that your key area of concern is around revenue development. You would like us to look into your domestic routes and carry out analysis on those that are not profitable. We should investigate opportunities for you to create revenue through the bundling of services, and outline and examine the approaches that other players have used to leverage on-line communities and social media. From a cost perspective,* *you would like us to investigate the simplification of administrative processes primarily in South America and South East Asia, as well as opportunities for you to further optimize your use of real estate.*

Provided that you are satisfied with the areas that we have identified together today, we will formulate a short proposal for a study outlining our approach in each area.

The consultants promise to deliver the proposal within five working days. The client thanks them for a productive discussion, and the meeting is concluded.

THE MEETING OUTCOME

Using a logic tree that was prepared based upon the consultants' knowledge of the domain and refined using inputs collected from the client, the consultants have succeeded in defining the scope and key priorities for a potential study that is aligned with the client's specific needs.

The diagram did not need to go into great detail to be useful in directing the discussion. Even if only highlighting the main areas of potential concern, the technique is helpful in prompting the client to comment on what is important and what is not, and provides the consultants with a good platform to navigate efficiently through the discussion. The technique also brings with it credibility, demonstrating a structured approach towards the task. This is more effective than starting with a blank sheet of paper and asking questions in a sequence that may appear somewhat random.

CHAPTER SUMMARY

Using a case study, this chapter has emphasized the importance of tailoring a consulting approach and the scope of any assignment to accurately address client-specific needs. In this case the logic-tree technique was used to direct the discussion.

When preparing the logic-tree diagram:

- Conduct a brainstorming session to build the tree as an initial hypothesis. Assemble a suitably qualified team within your organization when doing so.
- Give careful consideration to the definition of the main groups or branches of the tree. The approach should be complete, addressing the entire scope of the issue at hand, as well as logical and easy to follow.
- Be somewhat exhaustive in your thinking when populating the tree. Often causes that carry low probability are still included on the tree in order to demonstrate completeness in our approach.

When discussing the tree with the client:

- Be prepared to introduce the technique and explain how it will add value to the meeting: 'This is a simple way for us to break down your issue and identify the most critical causes quickly, thus saving time.'
- Navigate around the diagram in an appropriate order by taking a navigation check point so as to understand key priorities early in the discussion.
- Mark clear feedback onto the diagram as you proceed in your dialogue. The technique is visual in nature, and it is therefore preferable to bring the diagram to the meeting in an editable format. Use a notation that is clear, for example striking through items that are agreed to be out of scope, circling

those that are agreed to be in scope and using brackets for items that require further consideration off-line before a clear position can be reached.

- Agree upon clear priorities at the end of the session. If the study later has to be de-scoped due to a lack of time or budget, this information will become particularly important.

- Take good notes and provide an accurate summary at the end of your meeting that creates client confidence and a clear basis for moving forward.

PART III

ADDITIONAL TOPICS

CHAPTER FIVE

PROPOSING A CONSULTING SERVICE

Having established the objectives, scope and requirements associated with a potential consulting assignment, a written proposal will be submitted to the client containing an outline of the intended project, with accompanying commercial terms.

Proposal development calls upon the skill of good business writing and the careful selection of relevant content. For many assignments multiple consulting firms may be under consideration. A clear approach for achieving the assignment's objectives will therefore be required, emphasizing the credentials of the consulting firm and any differentiators that position it as an ideal partner to take on the work.

Chapter 1 contrasted the activities of consulting and selling and introduced the concept of consultative selling. Experience suggests that consultants who have gained a clear understanding of a client's needs through a structured dialogue and subsequently propose a well-tailored solution are likely to stand in a favourable position. Think about all of the information that you have collected in discussions with clients, both verbally and in documented form, and use it wisely.

Clients have reported a notable variation in the quality of the proposals that they receive from different firms. Some demonstrate a better understanding of their business needs than others; some consider the needs of all stakeholders concerned, whilst others do not; some proposals are structured, concise and easy to interpret, whilst others are verbose and include reference material of little relevance.

This chapter will outline some of the most important considerations during proposal development, suggesting items to include and practices to avoid.

SELECTING THE CONTENT

The content, structure and format of a proposal varies, depending upon the type of consulting service being offered. Some of the most common items included are elaborated below.

Executive summary

A good executive summary emphasizes the main messages contained within a proposal in just a few paragraphs. It is an important part of the proposal and is the only section that some senior executives may ever read. Others may use the summary as a basis for deciding whether or not to read the remainder of the document. The points included should link the client's ambitions with the proposed areas to be addressed, the obstacles to be overcome and the capabilities of the consulting company.

An example of an executive summary is presented in Chapter 8, *The Skill of Advising.*

Introductory chapter

An introductory chapter is generally used to create a relevant context for the proposal, generate interest in the mind of the reader and explain the structure of the remainder of the document. The title 'Introduction' is less commonly used in a proposal in favour of more meaningful titles such as 'The business opportunity' or 'The critical need for change', which bear relevance to the situation at hand. This section of the proposal should:

- Provide a clear background and explain why the assignment should be carried out. Reasons may relate to changes in industry regulations, competitive pressures or other issues of clear priority. Frame the problem to be solved or opportunity to be exploited clearly in the reader's mind.
- State clear business objectives for the assignment, including any associated measures, targets and timelines. These objectives will have been agreed in earlier client discussions and indicate the ambition level of the assignment.
- Refer to obstacles that will need to be overcome or factors that will be critical to the success of the assignment. This demonstrates forward thinking and provides a balanced view.
- Explain the format of the proposal, how it has been divided into sections and how the sections are intended to answer the reader's questions.

Approach

Outline the solution approach that will be proposed and explain why the chosen approach is optimal. Contrast it, if necessary, with other approaches that could have been pursued and present their relative pros and cons. Depending upon the type of assignment, supporting designs or solution descriptions may be required, together with an overview of the *methodology* that will be employed during the project.

The level of detail employed when documenting an approach should be a particular point of consideration. Consultants have a tendency to be conservative when sharing details of their intended approach. If too much detail is provided they fear that the client will take the proposal as an instruction manual and carry out the work themselves. An approach that is too thin, on the other hand, may fail to convey sufficient confidence and make it less likely that the proposal will be accepted. A balance between these extremes can be achieved by describing an approach as a sequence of activities, but without explaining in detail how each activity will carried out. This is usually sufficient to inspire client confidence without giving away too much intellectual property.

> *When describing your approach in a proposal, focus on the 'what', and not the 'how'.*

Time plan, deliverables and responsibilities

Usually presented in the form of a *Gantt chart*, the time plan illustrates the timing of different activities to be carried out during project execution. Milestones will have been defined corresponding to important events such as workshops where inputs will be gathered, meetings where work products will be reviewed, and the provision of finalized deliverables by the consulting team.

Deliverables may comprise documents, reports, presentations, workshops and a range of other items, depending upon the nature of the project. The intended content of each deliverable should be outlined clearly in the proposal. For certain types of deliverable the definition of *acceptance criteria* may also be required. A consulting firm delivering a complex IT solution, for example, will propose a set of acceptance criteria related to tests that will be conducted after implementation and criteria satisfied to demonstrate that their obligations have been fulfilled.

Responsibilities for both parties should be clearly outlined in the proposal document. A responsibility matrix is often drawn up for this purpose, listing the different tasks to be carried out and defining the responsibilities of the different parties and stakeholders. The *RACI* method is often used, where *R* denotes the party responsible for carrying out a task, *A* denotes the party responsible for approving completion of the task, *C* denotes parties who should be consulted during the execution of the task, and *I* denotes parties who should be kept informed on the progress of the task.

Pricing

Different commercial models can be used for the pricing of consulting services. Three of the most common are outlined below.

Fixed price   A fixed price is agreed for the provision of the service or solution. This is advantageous to the client as they have a fixed investment which is known upfront. It is advantageous to the consulting firm in situations where the project scope is clearly defined and parts of the work from previous projects can be reused. This enables the project to be delivered at a lower cost yet the firm is still able to charge the market price for the solution, resulting in increased profitability. If, on the other hand, the work required more effort than expected then the price to the client would not change and the consultants would be required to absorb any additional costs.

Time and materials   This is a common model for shorter consulting assignments and for assignments where the project's scope and duration are less clearly understood. When analysing a set of business processes, for example, consultants may not know the complexities that will be encountered from the start. Although an estimated level of effort will have been indicated, the consultants charge on an hourly basis for their services. If the work takes longer than estimated the client will pay for the additional hours up to an agreed maximum, and if it takes less time the client will pay less. *Materials* refers to any agreed expenses required during the execution of the project that will be charged in addition, such as travel expenses.

Shared risk, shared reward   If this model is applied, the consulting firm is paid based upon the business benefits enjoyed by the client as a result of the project. The model is less common and generally used in situations where there is a higher risk associated with the financial return against the project investment, or in cases where the return on investment is certain but the client has limited budget available to fund the project. A client commissioning the launch of a new service, for example, may be uncertain what the uptake in the market will be. Alternatively, a government agency may wish to undertake a project to improve tax collection processes but have limited spending available. In such cases a partial payment for the consulting service is usually made on a fixed-price basis in addition to a percentage of the financial benefits associated with the solution for a fixed time period.

Business benefits

Intended business benefits associated with the assignment – relating to items such as reduced costs, incremental revenues, reduced cycle times, improved measures of customer satisfaction – are generally described based upon the consultants' experience and results that have been achieved in previous projects. Whilst this provides the client with an important indication of the value that they should expect from the assignment, consultants prefer to contract against deliverables rather than business benefits. The reason is that whilst the deliverables produced are within the control of the consulting team, business benefits may be influenced by many external factors such as changes in the market or other events within the client organization.

In some cases it may be appropriate to include a business case in the proposal. If included the business case should emphasize:

- The financial impact of the issues to be addressed, or potential value of the opportunity to be exploited
- The cost of the investment and the expected return on investment
- The breakeven point when the cost of carrying out the assignment will have been recovered.

For a business case to be of value it must be tailored to the client's business through the incorporation of client-specific financial and performance measures collected during the pre-proposal dialogue. This was emphasized by a client in southern Europe.

'Some of the business cases that we receive in proposals are standard, based on previous projects that the consultants have conducted. They do not reflect the cost specifics or performance indicators of our business and are therefore not very meaningful.'

Credentials and references

Present good reasons why the consulting firm should be selected for the assignment. Some firms still employ the practice of including a standard three-page section in every proposal that presents their credentials. In the competitive world of business this is not advisable, and instead a more customized approach is preferred. You will need to document an argument describing why, for *this* assignment conducted for *this* client, your firm is the ideal choice. Information included may relate to:

- Similar projects that you have conducted successfully. These play an important role as they provide proof that you have the capability to do the work. If a reference case refers to the specifics of another client organization, their approval will be required before the information can be shared. For a reference case to carry weight the similarities between the previous project and the opportunity under discussion should be clear. Anonymous references carry little weight. Clients will often ask for the names of reference clients, and in some cases may ask for permission to contact them.
- Intellectual assets belonging to the consulting firm that can be reused. These may include industrialized solutions that can be customized, the results of analyses, methodologies, software, documentation and training materials.
- The calibre of the team that you have assembled for the project. Clients are aware that a strong and qualified team will play an instrumental role in the success of a project. Explain the intended team composition and include the profiles of staff who will assume key roles during the delivery phase.
- Client intimacy. When proposing new business to an existing client your knowledge of their organization and working practices will add value and enable the project team to get up to speed faster. This has been recognized as an advantage by a number of clients and is worth mentioning in the proposal.

Terms and conditions

Terms and conditions vary, depending upon type of assignment to be conducted, but may include the validity of the proposal (e.g. 30 days), payment terms and other conditions related to liabilities. Shorter consulting projects are often delivered based upon the sign-off of the proposal, hence the importance of including these terms. In the case of larger consulting projects a contracting exercise is usually conducted after proposal acceptance, and terms and conditions are handled as part of contracting.

PRACTICES TO AVOID

Common practices to avoid during proposal development relate to over-scoping, unrealistic commitments and the use of vague terminology.

Over-scoping

Consultants are eager to provide comprehensive and high-quality solutions. We like to be Rolls Royce designers. Nevertheless, it is important to respect the scope and priorities that have been articulated by the client. Additional elements can often be added into a proposal that add value, but these will also increase the scope of work and the cost of the project, and not every client wants to buy a Rolls Royce. Any items beyond the client's stated requirements should be included with caution and supported with clear argumentation if considered essential.

A consulting firm in the Netherlands was delighted to receive a request-for-proposal from an existing client in the banking industry. The consultants worked exhaustively on the proposal for two weeks and defined a comprehensive set of services to be delivered by a project team of 60 people over the course of a year. They finally submitted a well-written proposal and congratulated themselves, eager to hear their client's reaction. The next day they received a phone call from the client executive responsible for commissioning the work. 'I don't believe what I am reading!' he said. 'Why all of these people and all of these services? I was expecting a team of less than 20 for three months, initially. We asked you for an apple and you sent us a pumpkin!'

Experience has shown on many an occasion that the larger a potential project becomes in scope and duration, the more difficult it becomes to formulate and secure acceptance of the proposal. Consultancies therefore prefer to divide long-term engagements into smaller units of work that are aligned to a long-term vision and to propose them as incremental steps. This approach provides the client with more flexibility and the consultancy with a higher chance of proposal acceptance.

Unrealistic commitments

A proposal document aims to be persuasive in nature, and consultants are eager to ensure that their proposals are attractive. At the same time this eagerness can result in a tendency towards over-optimism. Trying to impress the client through the presentation of exaggerated capabilities, over-optimistic timelines or short-sighted commercial terms represents poor practice and can result a project commitments that will be impossible to deliver.

Whilst some clients are wary of consultants who make unrealistic commitments, others may encourage consultants to over-commit so that they can enforce financial penalties when deadlines are missed. Be wary of assuming that the consulting delivery team will find a way to catch up during the project. The cost of corrective actions may jeopardize the profitability of the work, and failures in delivery may damage the prospect of a long-term client relationship. This was emphasized by a project manager working in a large multinational organization.

> 'During the negation of a proposal our management always push our consulting suppliers on timelines. It is in their nature. The suppliers should handle this discussion delicately. Our management does not like to hear "no", but saying "yes" and then failing to deliver on time will create disappointment of a more serious nature.'

Vague terms

When developing a proposal, avoid the use of terms in that are open to different interpretations by different readers. In case of doubt, define your interpretation of relevant terms in a glossary that can be included as an appendix to the proposal.

A consulting firm had been contracted by a major bank to provide a financial risk management solution. The project ran for many months and was delivered successfully to its agreed timeline. Upon its conclusion, however, the client claimed that some of the reports that had been produced were incomplete. Further discussion revealed that the client had a different interpretation of the term 'risk management' than the consultants and had expected additional items to be covered. The result was several weeks of dispute and an amount of additional work.

CHAPTER SUMMARY

A strong consulting proposal has two principal objectives: First, to persuade the client to commission the work through the presentation of an attractive proposition; and second, to set realistic client expectations as to the project that will be delivered. For both of these objectives to be achieved a proposal team will be required that possesses appropriate knowledge of the consulting domain and content, sufficient skill to define a project with due consideration of time, resources and dependencies, and the ability to formulate appropriate commercial terms.

Consulting firms are rarely paid for proposal development activities, which puts them under pressure to create high-quality proposals whilst minimizing the time and cost required to do so. Having a clear strategy from the start of the proposal development process will save time and minimize work iterations. Make sure that your team members agree on the answers to two questions: 'What is our strategy for winning this assignment?' and 'What expectations must be properly set for the collaboration to succeed?' This will result in closer alignment, improved teamwork and a more cohesive proposal.

This chapter has discussed some of the most common topics included in proposals and highlighted some of the practices that should be avoided:

Over-scoping   Beware that some proposals become more about what the consultancy wants to sell than what the client wants to buy. This weakens the proposal in the eyes of the client and has caused many proposals to fail.

Unrealistic commitments   It is not unusual for consultants to take on challenging and in some cases stretching assignments, but agreeing to the unrealistic represents poor practice. Making additional promises may seem like an easy way to secure a deal, but avoid setting the delivery team up to fail.

Vague terms   Terms that could be open to different interpretations by different readers should be either avoided or clearly defined. Clients may otherwise be dissatisfied later in the engagement, or demand additional work to be performed without charge.

CHAPTER SIX

DELIVERING A CONSULTING SERVICE

Once a proposal has been accepted and contracting has been completed, the consulting engagement will move into its delivery phase. Consulting projects are often executed to tight timelines as clients are keen to secure the intended business benefits quickly. Consultants must therefore adopt an efficient approach during delivery, putting in place the required organization and processes to meet project goals with speed and accuracy. In addition, a suitable client collaboration approach will need to be adopted and tailored to the needs of the project. It is the skill of balancing these elements that ensures that project commitments are met and a high degree of client satisfaction is achieved. The importance of this was articulated by a senior manager at a financial institution in North America.

'Some consultancies are better at selling themselves than delivering. What happens in delivery is the real test and is the door-opener to future collaboration.'

Consulting projects generally involve a mix of client-facing and behind-the-scenes activities. In some cases a co-delivery approach may be employed where some activities are conducted by the consultants, others are conducted by the client team, and still others are conducted jointly. Close coordination between teams and clearly defined responsibilities are therefore imperative. Even with a well-defined delivery plan, obstacles and unexpected events will have to be handled, as well as any changes in the client's requirements as time progresses. Consultants should be skilled in handling such events with agility.

THE 50:50 RULE

> A business traveller is required to take a transatlantic flight lasting several hours to a meeting at a remote location. A number of international airlines have scheduled flights that would meet his needs. Travelling at short notice, he purchases an airline ticket, albeit at a premium price. On the day of the journey everything runs smoothly. The flight proceeds uneventfully, the aircraft lands five minutes ahead of schedule and his baggage is delivered punctually. His return journey two days later proceeds in a similar manner.
>
> Some weeks later he is required to travel to the same location and orders a second airline ticket. He receives a phone call from his travel agent. 'There are three different airlines offering good connections with equivalent prices', says the agent. 'Would you like to stay with the same airline, or select another?' Consider the basis of his decision...

A passenger purchasing the services of an airline is paying for the delivery of a specific *result*, namely arrival at their destination safely, punctually and complete with their checked baggage. The provision of this result constitutes fulfilment of the contract between the airline and the passenger. For many major transatlantic routes, however, there may be a number of airlines capable of delivering this result in a similar fashion.

Earning the favour of the client, particularly if regular business is to be conducted, will therefore require measures beyond the successful delivery of the result, measures that venture into the realm of the *client experience*. When asked by the agent, our traveller will probably think along the following lines:

'What was my experience with the airline last time? Was the aircraft clean and comfortable? Did my seat have sufficient leg room? How did the crew behave? Were they friendly, and did they treat me like a valued customer? Was a good selection of food and beverages offered? Were sufficient entertainment options available? And finally, if any issues arose during the delivery of the service, how were they handled? Perhaps it was difficult to find stowage space for my carry-on bag. Was the crew receptive and helpful in solving the problem, or did they leave me to search for a space? Overall, do I feel tempted to repeat the experience, or shall I select another airline for my next trip?'

The traveller's thoughts highlight one of the most fundamental principles related to the delivery of any service. Client satisfaction is driven by two key elements: Provision of the agreed result and the client experience delivered by the service provider. Both have a significant impact on the perception. In industries where high competition exists between many qualified providers, differentiation will need to be embedded in either or both of these elements, particularly if a price premium needs to be justified.

A passenger is likely to interact with the staff working on an airliner quite regularly during his or her trip and is therefore quite intimately involved in the service delivery experience. Consider a second example involving a different pattern of interaction.

A client engages two consulting firms to carry out different market-analysis tasks. Each firm is issued a brief detailing the requirements for their assignment, is invited to a meeting to discuss relevant details and has a period of three weeks to complete the work. The contracted deliverables are a presentation summarizing key findings and a report containing documented recommendations.

The first team of consultants meet with the client, having reviewed the brief. They are calm but somewhat rigid in their approach, clarify a few of the requirements and commit to providing the deliverables according to the proposed time plan. During the assignment little further communication takes place. The client feels somewhat concerned, hoping that the expected analysis will be delivered with accuracy. The day before their scheduled presentation the consultants contact the client to reconfirm their appointment. The presentation and report are delivered and the quality of the work is good. The client feels satisfied, and somewhat relieved.

The second team of consultants also meet with the client at the beginning of the assignment. They demonstrate a friendly and professional approach, building rapport with the client, acknowledging that they are pleased to have been selected for the work. In addition to seeking clarifications, they outline their intended approach, brief the client on the extended team that will contribute to the assignment, and propose to send a short status report at the end of each week. The final presentation and report delivered are both accurate and innovative.

Once the assignments have been completed, the client reflects upon the experience of working with two firms that undertook similar tasks and charged similar fees. The decision to engage the second firm for another upcoming assignment is not a difficult one. Even though the total amount of client interaction during the assignment amounted to less than two days during a three-week period, a different experience was delivered that had a distinct impact on client satisfaction.

Figure 6.1 introduces the concept of the *50:50 rule*, suggesting that during the delivery of a service 50% of client satisfaction is generated through the accurate provision of the agreed *result* and the remaining 50% is generated by the way in which the service was delivered and the resultant *client experience.*

Whilst the need to focus on the achievement of the contracted result is clear, the importance of optimizing the delivery experience is generally underestimated. What was it like to work with the consultants during the project? Did they engage in a way that created confidence? Did they craft an effective collaboration that maximized the value of their involvement? Were they a pleasure to have on the team?

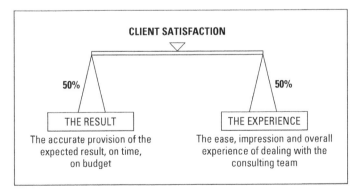

Figure 6.1: The 50:50 rule

The relative weight associated to each element could be argued and the 50:50 distribution is not an absolute, but rather based upon the experience of motivating the needed behaviours in consulting teams that are working to tight deadlines. Under pressure, these teams naturally focus on their deliverables and tend to neglect the daily practices required to optimize the client experience, potentially eroding the client relationship.

In highly competitive industries where a number of vendors are able to deliver similar results at a similar price the client experience can offer the greatest opportunity for differentiation. This is also where the personality of a consulting firm becomes apparent, which can strongly influence the possibility of future business. The importance of this was echoed by a senior executive in a technology company.

> 'When we select a consulting company for a particular assignment there are usually at least five different firms that we could consider, firms that are suitably qualified to undertake the assignment. Their fees, at least after negotiation, land at fairly similar levels. The real question to us, therefore, is which firm will be a good partner to work with for the next six months? A firm that will send us a good team, engage well with the people in our organization, be a pleasure to have in-house and work closely with us on a daily basis to resolve problems.
>
> We evaluate this based upon two factors. For companies that we have worked with before we consider our experience in previous project deliveries. And for companies that we are considering for the first time, we pay careful attention to their behaviour in initial meetings and proposal discussions, the accuracy and timeliness of their responses, and so forth. The way that a vendor behaves during initial discussions is a very good indicator as to how they will behave during project delivery.'

In summary, two mechanisms need to be working in order to maximize client satisfaction during the delivery of a consulting assignment: one that knows how to deliver projects with high accuracy, meet deadlines and navigate around obstacles on the way; and one that knows how to manage the client and the overall delivery experience resulting in a rich collaboration. The remainder of this chapter will discuss these two mechanisms in further detail.

DELIVERING THE RESULT

The detailed approaches used in the delivery of a consulting assignment vary according to the nature of the assignment, the activity domain and the results that the assignment is expected to deliver. The approach required to conduct a market analysis, for example, clearly differs from that required to evaluate and optimize a set of business processes within an organization. Regardless of these specifics, a structured approach or *methodology* will be required, a suitable project organization defined and measures put in place to ensure that the assignment is successfully launched and managed through to completion.

Consulting methodologies

A variety of methodologies are used in the consulting industry, each specific to the type of assignment to be carried out. Some methodologies are used on an industry-wide basis, whereas others may be proprietary to a particular consulting firm, highly developed and part of their unique proposition. In either case the methodology is intended to provide an overall structure for the assignment and generally consists of two components: A *roadmap* illustrating the steps required to navigate from point A to point B; and a set of *tools* and *templates* that may be required along the way.

The roadmap component graphically divides an assignment into phases, defines the activities to be carried out within each, suggests milestones for the synchronization of different activities and includes check points to ensure quality and effective governance. Documented guidelines are also provided for each of the activities to be carried out.

Figure 6.2 illustrates a simplified methodology that divides an assignment into five phases, beginning with the collection of client requirements and ending with the handover of a solution to the client organization. Within each phase there are defined activities to be carried out and a check point taken to ensure that all activities have been successfully completed before the next phase begins. The use of check points is common in methodologies to ensure that omissions early in an assignment do not turn into serious issues at a later stage.

The tools accompanying the methodology support the activities to be carried out within each phase. If a business case needs to be formulated during the requirements analysis phase, then a tool or spreadsheet may be provided that contains the required formulas and layout. Document templates are also included to support accurate information gathering, analysis and decision-making as well as to ensure that documentation is created in a consistent manner. The inclusion of these items promotes quality and saves time as consultants will not need to re-create tools and templates as part of every project.

Good methodologies evolve over time and embody lessons learned from earlier projects. The developers of methodologies observe patterns of issues that projects have encountered, the way in which obstacles have been overcome, and subsequently embed this thinking into the methodology for the benefit of future teams. As a result, the documented guidelines associated with a methodology can be a valuable learning tool, particularly for junior staff who may have limited project experience.

Methodologies provide a consistent set of vocabulary for use by project team members through the naming of different phases, activities and check points. If a project manager said 'We are about to begin the solution design phase' or 'We have just passed decision gate 2', staff joining the project would understand the stage of progress, the activities that have been

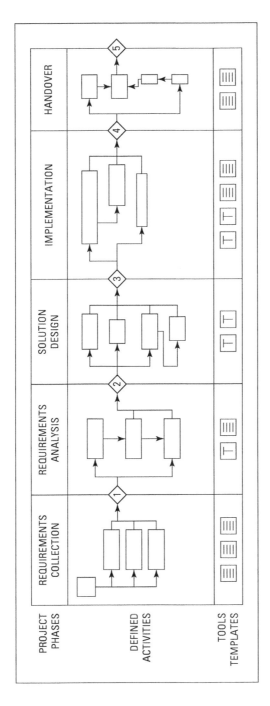

Figure 6.2: Methodology example

completed and the probable next steps through their knowledge of the methodology.

Methodologies are usually scalable so that they can be applied effectively by large and small projects alike. Only the core parts of the methodology are usually classified as mandatory, with other detailed activities and guidelines included on an optional basis. This allows a methodology to add structure and the benefit of lessons learned without hampering creativity. A small team executing a consulting project lasting for only two weeks may choose to follow only the mandatory governance structure and check points of the methodology, whereas a project lasting for six months with a large team may find it useful to utilize all defined activities and guidelines at the detailed level.

Good judgement is fundamental to applying methodology in an optimal way, as is the ability to decide when to follow the guidance of a methodology and when to depart from it. Methodologies are based upon best practice and what has succeeded in the past. Best practice works in many places but not everywhere, and every situation is unique.

The project organization

The successful delivery of a consulting project will require a team of consultants, often referred to as *resources*, suitable in skill and sufficient in number to conduct the project that has been contracted. Collectively referred to as the *project organization*, they will be led by a project manager responsible for ensuring that all project deliverables are produced according to the agreed timeline and allocated budget. In larger projects the resources may be further divided into teams with specific responsibilities, each led by a team leader reporting to the project manager. Projects that involve both consultant and client participation will be manned by teams from both parties, as illustrated by the project organization chart in Figure 6.3. Other *sponsors* from either organization who do not have day-to-day

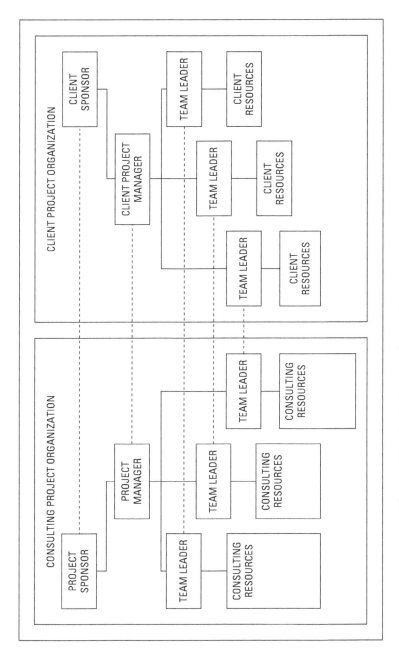

Figure 6.3: Typical consultant/client project organization

project responsibilities but have senior-level authority and a commercial interest in the project may also be depicted on the organization chart.

The amount of client interaction required within a project will depend upon the nature of the work being done. Project members should be briefed clearly on any client interactions that they are expected to direct. The project manager and team leaders will usually represent the main client interfaces.

During project execution it is often practical for the consultants to do the majority of their work in their own offices and for client interaction to take place in the form of meetings, some of which may be periodic and others scheduled as required. This approach brings with it a number of advantages:

- The consulting firm will have a great deal of flexibility regarding the way in which the project is staffed and how tasks are assigned to different individuals. Junior consultants who are not client-facing may also contribute to the work, or shadow other staff for learning purposes.
- Tasks may be delegated to geographically dispersed or off-shore teams, a model that is becoming increasingly common in large consulting organizations. One reason to adopt this approach is to utilize different time zones, enabling work to continue around the clock in response to tight deadlines. Another reason to off-shore, particularly in mature global markets, is to reduce project delivery costs by leveraging lower resource costs overseas. The approach can, however, bring with it some challenges.

A project based in Europe had a team working from 9.00 a.m. until 5.00 p.m. each day. At 4.00 p.m. they would hand over their work to a team of colleagues at one of their North American offices who would continue to work on the project deliverables. At 4.00 p.m. in North America the work was handed over to a team in Asia that would work for another eight hours before subsequently handing the work back to Europe. Some tasks involved the participation of team members from all sites. Other tasks, less suited to development by several resources, were split between the sites for parallel development. When producing a document, for example, each site was given the responsibility to develop a clearly defined chapter and then the chapters were assembled and reviewed as a cohesive deliverable. Whilst this approach continued for several weeks and enabled an aggressive deadline to be met, the associated challenges should not be underestimated. Seamless cross-site collaboration is harder to achieve in practice than in theory, which was reflected in the findings of a review conducted at the project's conclusion. Teams had to be very well synchronized. To achieve this some resources had to travel between project sites, resulting in additional costs. Furthermore, a lot of time was taken up in the daily handovers, reworking was often required when remote teams had not understood their tasks correctly or lacked the skills to do them, and it was difficult to schedule phone conferences involving all three teams due to time conflicts.

In other situations when close client collaboration is required it may be less appropriate for the consultants to run a project in-house. The consulting team may then be relocated onto the client's premises for the duration of the project, commonly referred to as *working on client site*. The consultant and client teams then work alongside each other and in some cases joint client–consultant teams may be formed. The formulation of a joint team can expedite the leverage of both consultant and client knowledge and is often used as a mechanism to increase the transfer of knowledge during a project. Keep in mind that when a consulting team is located on site, every consultant becomes a potential client interface. Whilst clients will have been informed as to their principal interfaces, in practice they may approach any consultant on the team. All consulting resources should therefore be briefed on the handling of questions and client requests, information that can be shared and the handling of intellectual property proprietary to the consulting organization.

A consulting team worked at a client's premises for several months in Switzerland. The team of 25 consultants shared an open-plan office with approximately 40 client personnel, collaborating fluidly on a daily basis. As time progressed, however, the intended communication approach began to break down. Instead of approaching the designated points of contact for particular questions, the client team members approached other members of the consulting team whom they knew well or the consultant sitting nearest to them. Frequent miscommunications occurred as only the dedicated interfaces within the consulting team were in possession of the latest, up-to-date information.

Client team members also began approaching the consultants with requests for assistance beyond the agreed project scope. The consulting team members had been instructed to politely decline such requests or to redirect them to the project manager, but in response the client personnel would present the same question to several consultants until someone eventually agreed to help.

This situation is not unique and emphasizes the importance of ensuring that consultants working on site understand the scope of their responsibilities and are able to direct communication appropriately. Working on site provides an excellent opportunity to collaborate with clients and build good knowledge of the client organization. However, if a project is to progress efficiently the rules of engagement must be clear.

Consulting firms have choices as to how they construct an optimal organization for each project, and different approaches have their pros and cons. Some clients express a preference for on-site collaboration whilst others are indifferent. These choices will impact on the client delivery experience, and working practices may need to be adjusted to ensure that perceptions are correctly managed. This was illustrated by the comments of an executive at a leading corporation in North America.

'We are working with two large consulting firms to upgrade business support systems in different parts of our organization. Both companies are performing well, although their project approaches are somewhat different. The first company has embedded 20 people in our office for the duration of the project, and we see consultants running around on a daily basis. The second company does most of the work from their office and at remote delivery centres located around the globe. Their people come here and meet with us a few times each week then return to their office and get on with the job. Both companies deliver good quality and meet their deadlines. The interesting thing, however, is at the end of the month when we receive an invoice from each company. The invoices are for large figures as a lot of work has been done, but somehow we find the invoice from the first supplier easier to approve. It seems that the experience of seeing people working in front of you gives the perception of value.'

Such comments have been made by other clients and provide an interesting insight into their perceptions. Whilst the second consulting firm was probably able to deliver their project at a lower cost through the use of remote delivery methods, a negative impact on the client's perception had resulted. To prevent this it is important to ensure that those working at the client interface are skilled in updating the client and emphasizing what is going on behind the scenes to provide the same perception of value.

The internal launch meeting

The launch of a consulting project brings with it the need to mobilize a delivery team, bring people up to speed quickly, have them assume their roles and get to work on their tasks. A common way to achieve this is by conducting an internal project launch meeting. Usually led by the project manager, the meeting is generally attended by all assigned consultants as well as other internal stakeholders who have an interest in the project.

The objectives of this meeting are to:

- *Assimilate* the team, sharing the project background
- Present the planned *delivery strategy*, principal activities and timeline
- Secure the team's *commitment*, answer questions and address concerns.

Assimilating the team

A well-assimilated team will be in a better position to work efficiently, will require less support and will be more knowledgeable and credible in front of the client. The internal launch meeting provides an excellent opportunity to brief your team before they embark on the project and is helpful in providing a holistic view, particularly if some team members will only work on certain tasks or deliverables. The content presented during the meeting should be selected carefully. Common items include:

The client's business   Highlights of the client's business (as described in Chapter 2, *Preparing to Consult*), with a particular focus on current business direction, ambitions and challenges. Connect the information presented, where possible, to the business background of the project to be executed. Be sure to answer the question: 'Why is the client conducting this project?'

Project objectives, scope and deliverables   Present the stated objectives of the project, the project scope to be addressed and the deliverables to be produced (e.g. reports, presentations, designs, software, training packages).

Project stakeholders   Outline the stakeholders who will be involved from both the client and consulting organizations. A stakeholder is typically defined as anyone who can either positively or negatively impact the outcome of the project. How do the client stakeholders view the project? Are they likely to be positive collaborators, or is resistance or poor cooperation anticipated?

Responsibilities   Responsibilities should have been clearly defined for both the consultant and client organizations in the consulting proposal or contract. Ensure that all consultants have an understanding of these commitments. Responsibilities at team level should also be discussed.

Risks   Prior to accepting an assignment, it is common for consulting firms to define a list of risks to be managed during the delivery of the project, a topic that will be elaborated later in this chapter. Sharing risk-related information during the internal launch meeting is good practice and enables the whole team to contribute to risk-monitoring activities. This responsibility should not rest with the project manager alone.

Tools and methodologies   The consulting team should be briefed on the specific tools and methodologies that will be used during the project. Clients may have requested the use of specific tools for the preparation of documents, presentations or other deliverables that are compatible with the tools used in their own organization.

Logistics Particularly for projects that will be conducted on site, logistics-related information should be shared on travel and administration policies, security procedures, access to offices, and so forth.

Outlining the project delivery strategy

Having presented the project background, it will be important to outline the intended delivery strategy. Common items include the following:

The project plan The project plan will include the project timeline, key activities and milestones. Consulting projects are often executed to tight timelines, which may appear unfeasible at first sight unless a suitable delivery strategy is clearly presented. Explain how the progress of tasks will be optimized, how certain activities will be carried out in parallel, outline content that will be reused from previous projects and highlight any bottleneck periods close to deadlines when the team may need to be on standby to put in additional effort.

Client inputs and dependencies The client may have agreed to provide additional inputs at defined points during the project. Client teams running other projects often create these inputs, commonly referred to as *input deliverables*, which in turn constitute dependencies that must be managed. Contingency plans are often built into the project plan related to these and should be outlined to the team: 'In the event that the client experiences delays and provides the phase 2 inputs late, this is how we will reschedule project activities to minimize the impact.'

The project organization Present the project organization chart describing the definition of teams and principal client interfaces.

Securing the team's commitment

Team commitment relates to the human factor of an internal launch meeting. The meeting should be a team-building activity and a motivational experience. Ensure that the team members view the project as a good opportunity to deliver an interesting assignment and to learn something along the way. Consulting firms ask for both commitment and flexibility from their people, but ultimately resources will ask themselves the question 'What's in it for me?' Highlight opportunities for team members to develop professionally during the project, either through the acquisition of new skills or by broadening their experience. This can have a positive effect on both individual motivation and team morale. A well-assimilated and highly motivated delivery team will create a much more favourable impression when meeting client stakeholders for the first time. This was emphasized by a senior manager based in the Netherlands, based upon his experience of supervising projects delivered by a number of consulting firms.

'We have dealt with many companies and the experience has been quite diverse. We have worked with consulting teams who arrive on day 1 of the project well prepared. They understand what they are there to do, get to work quickly and are a pleasure to have in-house. Deadlines are often tight, but they work efficiently like a well-oiled machine and even demonstrate high spirits while doing so. They deliver good work in limited time and set a good example to my staff. These are the kind of consultants that we do not hesitate to engage again.

Other consulting teams have given us quite the opposite experience. They arrive on site as a group of individuals who have apparently been assembled for the project at the last minute. They spend most of their first week reading documentation and talking about the task ahead. I think to myself: "Did they not prepare beforehand? Are we paying for this?" They are somewhat chaotic, with selected individuals working very long nights close to deadlines. We wonder if they will deliver on time and with high quality. These are the kind of consultants we would only call back if they bring specific skills that are hard to find in the marketplace. They do the job, but they don't inspire confidence.'

OPTIMIZING THE CLIENT EXPERIENCE

During the delivery of a consulting project active steps should be taken to ensure that the client experience is optimized. These relate principally to the establishment of suitable client relationships at all project levels, ensuring that these relationships are maintained, and directing communication concerning any issues that arise in an appropriate manner.

Building the client relationship

All consultants working at the client interface should consider themselves relationship managers. Good working relationships are an important enabler for the value that consultants can add. They secure the cooperation needed during a consulting project and enhance the consultant's understanding of the organization with which he or she is working. Consultants have choices as to the style of relationships that they build with their clients. These should be based upon conscious decisions, as should the actions that accompany them, as notably different outcomes will result. The personalities of the clients with whom relationships are to be built should also be considered: some clients may be formal in their approach, whilst others may prefer a more informal style. For discussion purposes we will classify client relationships at two extremes: the *transactional* relationship versus the *partner-oriented* relationship. Each of these relationships has distinct characteristics and we will examine the merits of each.

The transactional relationship

The transactional relationship is the simplest type of relationship that can be conducted between two parties and keeps the amount of contact and communication to the minimum required to achieve the result. Transactional relationships are effective in situations where infrequent communication is required between the parties for the result to be achieved and where the responsibilities of each party are clearly defined.

> A tourist visiting a foreign city walks into an event kiosk to purchase a concert ticket. He briefly exchanges courtesies with the agent and specifies the ticket that he wants to buy. He asks a few questions regarding the concert and the agent provides simple, although limited answers. His payment is processed and he leaves the kiosk moments later holding the ticket.

A transactional relationship is fast and effective, provided that the client clearly specifies what he requires and the agent executes his responsibilities correctly. A business transaction is completed with the minimum amount of overhead. The resulting relationship is, however, limited in depth. If the tourist above returns a week later to buy a second ticket and meets the same agent, the agent may not remember him. The relationship is also limited in scope: if the agent were asked a question beyond his immediate knowledge he would most likely state that he is unable to help rather than to try to find an answer through alternative means. And the relationship brings with it little tolerance: If the agent had made a mistake such as issuing the wrong ticket or charging the wrong price the tourist might quickly have become irritated. In this example, however, the advantages and limitations of the relationship balance in a way that is suited to the task at hand.

The partner-oriented relationship

Consulting is delivered as a high-value service, and during a project consultants are likely to interact with client personnel on a more regular basis. Aiming to position ourselves in the role of a partner, the required relationships will extend beyond transactional qualities. The creation of a partner-oriented relationship will require the investment of additional effort, usually related to simple practices, to craft a relationship of greater longevity and with notably different characteristics. Such relationships are built over time; however, early actions play an important role in shaping them.

> Consider how you would behave towards a newly employed colleague at your work place, assigned as a member of your team. On her first day you would probably greet your colleague enthusiastically, taking the time to talk with her and getting to know her on a professional level. You may decide to brief her on your role and the tasks that you are working on, suggesting ways in which you will be able to collaborate moving forward. And you may invite her to approach you should she have questions as she gets to work on her assigned tasks.

Relationships with clients and colleagues clearly differ, but when seeking to establish a partner-oriented relationship some similarities can be observed. Typical practices that are employed by consultants when establishing new client relationships include:

- Ensuring that a positive impression is made on clients, thorough preparation and a well-organized approach
- Demonstrating a friendly and constructive attitude in order to be recognized as someone who will be a pleasure to work with

- Taking the time to explain their roles, intended ways of working, and how they will approach project tasks to ensure favourable outcomes. This gives clients an understanding of what to expect, and the types of questions they can pose
- Seeking to understand their clients, their roles and associated working approaches. Gauging how clients feel about the consulting project, the potential benefits that it will bring to their organization and any concerns that they may have.

Making simple efforts such as these will contribute to the creation of a partner-oriented relationship that embodies, in particular, the following characteristics:

- A *better understanding* of the people and organizations that you are consulting for. Insights shared by clients during your dialogue will provide a clearer view of the assignment context. The thinking behind the client's requirements will become more evident and potential concerns will become easier to anticipate.
- You are likely to benefit from *increased cooperation*. When a good relationship has been established, clients tend to answer questions and share information more freely, as well as volunteering information that they feel may be useful.
- *Additional flexibility.* In the real world of business even skilled professionals make mistakes. If a partner-oriented relationship has been established an error does not usually erode the client relationship immediately. Clients are more inclined to respond: 'Your work is usually very good. Please fix this, and try to make sure that it doesn't happen again. Let's get on with the project'.

The effort invested in building a partner-oriented relationship increases the value that we are in a position to add and helps to navigate around some of the issues and obstacles that we may face. This was articulated by a senior manager in a consulting organization.

'I am responsible for a consulting team that has supported a large client with innovation and product development for the last few years. We have delivered some good projects and we have some good achievements behind us, but there is an element of risk associated with our work and there have also been less successful projects. In the less successful cases it is the relationship with our client that has always saved us. There is a good understanding between the client and consultant teams, the client knows that our approach is robust and that our team is committed. This continues to drive the success of our collaboration.'

Maintaining the relationship

Having established a partner-oriented relationship, consideration should be given to how the relationship will be maintained and evolved over time. Relationships may get off to a good start but in some projects consultants have been known to slip back into transactional mode and the relationship has been eroded. To avoid this the following points are worthy of particular attention:

Continued professionalism   Continue to demonstrate a professional approach throughout your interactions. The style of the relationship may become less formal through familiarity, but the level of professionalism demonstrated should not diminish. Do not get sloppy just because you have a good relationship with the client, arrive late at meetings, slip on deadlines or become too comfortable as you feel that there will be few consequences. An appropriate level of respect must be maintained through a structured, organized and detail-oriented approach to your work. A consultant is a guest in the client's business, and this requires some etiquette, as when you are a guest in someone's house. Demonstrate courtesy towards other client personnel, even towards those with whom you have no interaction, and avoid making unnecessary complaints about client facilities or other environmental factors, even if they are less than ideal.

Sharing your delivery strategy When a consulting project is proposed a high-level delivery strategy will be presented to the client, explaining how the objectives of the assignment will be addressed and the required deliverables created. During the early stages of delivery this approach is usually refined and elaborated to a more detailed level. Creative delivery strategies are often required behind the scenes to address tight timelines. These constitute part of the 'magic' that enables consultants to deliver high-quality solutions within short time periods. An interesting question is how much of the detailed delivery approach should be shared with the client. The sharing of excessive detail about internal work methods is usually undesirable, may complicate matters and limit flexibility. It is, however, important that the client has a sufficient understanding of the mechanisms that are in place to ensure project success. Ensure that any relevant points regarding the ongoing delivery strategy are communicated and apply good judgement. Avoid the situation where the client is losing sleep, wondering how the consultants will meet their deadlines, when everything is actually under control.

Keeping the client informed During the delivery phase, project status reports will be produced at an agreed frequency, for example at the end of each week. The reports will describe the status of tasks and the values of performance indicators that have been defined to measure project progress. Even with this type of reporting mechanism in place, consultants may need to provide additional status updates to clients in response to a variety of factors. Close to a critical deadline, for example, clients may appreciate daily updates explaining how last-minute issues are being handled, or if a serious problem arises during the project clients may appreciate hourly updates until the matter has been resolved. The personalities of client stakeholders also play a role, some clients being more hands-off and others more hands-on, and judgement may be required to adapt the approach accordingly. If your client is approaching you too often with the question 'What is the status?', this should raise a red flag and a question in your mind: Are you keeping them sufficiently informed to maintain confidence and satisfaction?

A senior consultant was delivering a project for a large pharmaceutical company in Western Europe. Her team reported to a director in the client organization, a woman with high standards and a reputation for ensuring good performance from the projects that she supervised. From the inception of the project the consultants noticed that the client always seemed to be stressed. She would call them once or twice each day, enquiring about the status of different tasks. The consultants were always able to reassure the client that everything was on track as detailed in the weekly reports, but day after day the questions continued to come. The senior consultant eventually raised this point with her team. 'This is not the type of relationship we aim to have with our clients', she said. 'Perhaps we should reconsider the way that we communicate with our client stakeholder.'

On giving the matter further consideration, the team realized that the stakeholder concerned was responsible for a number of simultaneous projects being delivered by different consultancy firms. She probably spent a good part of each day calling different project managers with similar questions to ensure that there would be no delays in their deliveries. They decided to take a proactive step and adjust their communication approach by sending a brief informal status report to the client via email at the end of each day.

> The email would summarize the tasks that had been completed, the tasks planned for the following day and the status on any ongoing issues. The change in client behaviour that resulted was quite remarkable. Not only did the questions stop coming, but at project meetings the client often began to comment: 'I like you guys. You are the ones that I don't have to worry about.'

Professional distance

When consultants work with clients for a prolonged period of time it is inevitable that a social element will develop within the relationship. You may find yourself drinking coffee with the client, going to lunch and even attending after-work social events. Whilst this can be healthy in a good business relationship, you may also need to consider how a suitable level of professional distance will be maintained, respecting the associated guidelines of your organization. Your primary role remains to represent the business relationship between the consulting firm and the client organization. If your personal relationship with a client should overtake this, conflicts are likely to result. The rules of engagement in personal and professional relationships differ, particularly with regard to the way that favours are granted. Your client might call and say, for example, 'I have a lot of questions regarding the new system that your company has delivered. I know that you must have an internal document containing the details that interest me. Could you share it unofficially?' or 'I know that the findings of your analysis will be announced on Friday. Could you give me an unofficial preview of the result?' In a professional business relationship either of these requests would require approval by management in the consulting organization, otherwise they would need to be politely declined. If a relationship has become too personal, however, you may face more pressure.

Build good relationships with clients, but always act as an ambassador for your organization.

Dealing with issues

Consulting projects tend to revolve around complex, business-critical matters, and there are a number of issues and unexpected events that can occur as a project progresses. A project that experiences no issues from start to finish is quite a rarity, and consultants should therefore expect and be equipped to deal with this. When classifying issues it is common to distinguish *internal issues* that arise as a result of processes within the consulting organization from *external issues* that are driven by the client or factors in the external environment (Figure 6.4). These two types of issue require different approaches and can be influenced to differing degrees.

Internal issues relate to events within the consulting organization that could threaten the successful and timely delivery of a project. Staff members intended to assume important roles may become unavailable, either due to the extension of existing assignments or due to unexpected illness; support promised by other internal teams may not be provided as expected, or it may

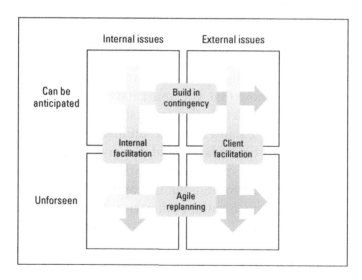

Figure 6.4: Classification of issues

emerge that the time and effort allocated to certain tasks were underestimated.

External issues may relate to changing circumstances within the client organization. Client stakeholders may leave their positions and their replacements may have different views on the project approach; the client team may fail to provide the level of cooperation that was initially agreed, or dependencies with other client initiatives may cause delays or other impacts. Other factors in the external environment may need to be considered such as travel irregularities that prevent staff from attending project meetings or delay the transit of equipment and other resources.

Issues can be further broken down according to whether they can be *anticipated* or are *unforeseen* and arise without warning. The mechanisms for dealing with these types of issue are quite different.

The ability to manage and ultimately resolve an issue relies on the skills and experience of the consulting team, their ability to leverage the experience of other colleagues and the prudent use of lessons learned from earlier projects.

Internal issues

Internal facilitation within the consulting organization is often required to address an internal issue by engaging stakeholders or other internal units that have the capacity to provide support. The ability to facilitate internally is of particular importance in larger consulting organizations, and a clear set of facilitation or escalation procedures should be available to engage stakeholders who have the authority to approve out-of-the-ordinary actions at short notice. A project located in Northern Europe that is missing staff members due to a flu epidemic may need, for example, to utilize an internal procedure to fly in colleagues from its Southern European hub to keep the project on track.

A senior consultant was assigned to manage a project team in South East Asia who were implementing a database solution for a client in the media industry. The client had stipulated a strict timeline of six months for the project, tied to the intended launch of a new service in their marketplace. Internally within the consulting firm the success of this project relied upon the careful coordination of three teams: a local implementation and training team; A remote team located in France responsible for the development of user applications; and a team located in Germany responsible for the manufacture and supply of specialized equipment.

Six weeks into the project an unexpected issue arose. A fire broke out in the factory in Germany, resulting in shipping delays of up to two months on all orders. The project manager realized that with this delay there was no possibility of achieving the project deadline and of the client launching their new service as planned. He did not relish the idea of sharing this news with the client, who had already reserved advertising slots for the launch on local television channels. After giving the matter some consideration he invoked an internal escalation procedure to engage the department at his head office that had ultimate authority over the order queue. It emerged that four of the required units were scheduled for dispatch during the month of July and it was possible to arrange for deliveries to be reprioritized with only minor impacts on the other ordering projects. This action minimized the potential delay in delivery to just two weeks. The project manager then adjusted his own project plan by rescheduling some planned training sessions for client staff to earlier dates. Once the training sessions had been completed, technical experts could be freed up to accelerate final implementation and testing tasks. As a result of these measures, the project delivered on time, yielding a successful launch and a high degree of client satisfaction.

In addition to the use of issue-handling procedures, contacts and personal networks can play an instrumental role in the ability to facilitate effectively in large organizations. This was echoed by a senior manager working at one of the South American hubs of a major airline.

'I have been based in South America for quite some years, responsible for day-to-day operations as well as the implementation of any changes to our local procedures. Two years ago I requested a temporary relocation for six months and accepted an assignment at our headquarters in Europe. The assignment was interesting, but what I really wanted to learn was how decisions are made at headquarters, how the different departments interact, and to meet some of the departmental heads. Now back at my home location life is much easier. I have a better understanding of how things work in the company as a whole, and have a good network of contacts to call on, in addition to our usual procedures, if we need something to be approved quickly.'

External issues

The resolution of an external issue will often require an element of client facilitation, particularly if the issue originates from within the client organization. Client-driven issues often fall contractually beyond the scope of consultants' responsibilities but can nevertheless affect the success of the project as a whole. When these issues arise it is usually pertinent to engage the client organization as early as possible, either to motivate the required cooperation or to escalate the matter to client decision-makers.

If the client team fails to provide a document containing important inputs at an agreed project milestone, for example, this may cause a subsequent delay in the consultants' work.

The consultants' first course of action would be to contact the responsible client team, emphasizing the importance of the inputs and asking for the situation to be addressed with urgency. If the client team still failed to respond then a second course of action would be for the responsible consulting manager to escalate the matter to the project sponsor within the client organization. The course of action that is generally least advisable when dealing with a client-driven issue is to *sit back and do nothing*. Good communication around the issue-handling process is an important part of a partner-oriented relationship, as highlighted by the example below.

A consulting team was delivering a project for a leading telecommunications company in Scandinavia. The project was divided into three phases, each requiring design activities to be carried out based upon specifications provided by client teams. The first and second phases of the project were completed successfully, but when the third phase began one of the client teams failed to provide their specification on the agreed date. The consultants' initial position on this issue was to wait for the inputs to arrive. Although the missing specifications were likely to cause a delay, they felt that the matter was beyond their control and beyond their contractual obligation. They sent reminders to the client team periodically but to no avail. Finally, after three weeks, the project manager escalated the matter to the client sponsor. His response was one of frustration.

'As a partner I expect you to make sure that your engagement with my organization is successful', he said. 'If my people are not cooperating then I would expect you, as a partner, to either push them or to contact me as early as possible so that I can take action. A project delay of three weeks due to a cooperation issue is unacceptable!'

Escalation within the client organization is generally reserved as a last resort as it can cause erosion to daily working relationships. Whilst it is preferable to solve problems on the ground, escalation will sometimes be required. The resolution of client-driven issues may not be our primary responsibility but still requires our vigilance. In a partner-oriented relationship the goal is not simply for us to fulfil our contracted responsibilities, but also to ensure that the overall project is successful.

Issues that can be anticipated

Issues that can be anticipated are usually addressed through the identification of project-related *risks* before the project begins. A risk, in this context, is something that experience suggests could go wrong during the project, but is not a certainty. When planning a project it is usual for the consulting team to make a list of risks and to identify corresponding actions that could be used to mitigate them. Later if a risk comes to pass then it will be reclassified as an issue.

'When planning a walk on a particular day you may know that it might rain. This brings with it a risk, although not a certainty, of getting wet. But if you eventually do get wet this is something that you may consider to be an issue. To mitigate the risk therefore, you may decide to carry an umbrella.'

Not all risks that are identified by a project team are likely to be mitigated. This decision is based upon the probability associated with each risk, the cost of mitigation and the severity of the impact if the issue transpires. In our simple example, if you feel that getting wet has little consequence you may decide not to carry an umbrella. For some risks several different mitigation options may be considered. For others mitigation may be either complex or impossible. The risk would then simply be monitored and the issue handled if it arises.

A consulting firm had been engaged to develop an industrial automation solution. A small part of the project required specialist knowledge and it had been agreed that this work would be subcontracted to a small overseas vendor, able to provide the specialist skills. Acting in a prime role, however, the consulting firm was responsible for the delivery of the overall solution. The consultants recognized that any delay in the work of the subcontractor would result in failure to meet the project deadline. Never having worked with the vendor before, they defined this as a project risk and considered their mitigation options.

The first option was not to mitigate the risk at all and to hope that the vendor would deliver on time. Should the vendor deliver late, however, they would have to deal with the associated consequences.

The second option was to mitigate the risk by monitoring the vendor with increased frequency, scheduling additional status meetings and bearing the cost of the additional overhead.

The third and most elaborate option was to mitigate the risk by flying one of their project managers overseas to work alongside the vendor for the four-week duration of their involvement in order to ensure on-time delivery, albeit with the highest associated cost.

They evaluated these alternatives carefully and opted for the second approach, bearing in mind the good reputation of the subcontracted vendor.

Issues that are difficult to foresee

Issues that are difficult to foresee will have to be addressed as they occur. Timely reaction and the attention of skilled staff are instrumental to expediting the resolution of such issues. For this reason large consulting projects often dedicate a small team of specialists to issue resolution during the delivery phase. This team will prioritize the issues according to their business impacts, focus on issue resolution, and in some cases identify temporary work-around solutions if an issue cannot be resolved immediately.

Most mature clients understand that issues are likely to occur during a project and evaluate consultants carefully based upon their behaviour around the issue-handling process. Consistent with our earlier discussion of the 50:50 rule, this evaluation is based upon not only the consultants' ability to resolve the issues but also the experience of working with them during the process.

A leading IT provider was engaged to implement a set of business-critical systems for a large corporation in South America. The project, lasting several months, was complex as the systems under implementation were highly customised and included a number of innovative features. Although the project succeeded in delivering on time, there were a number of outstanding technical issues upon project completion. The most serious of these related to the performance of the system, which was operating at only half the intended speed. This issue was causing substantial inconvenience to the people in the client organization who were forced to manage backlogs and were unable to retire the older systems that had been replaced. A team of internal specialists was brought in from the headquarters of the consulting company to expedite the resolution of the situation. One of their tasks was to meet with the client sponsor and attempt to repair a client relationship that was likely to have been eroded. On the morning of their meeting with the sponsor they were prepared for a somewhat hostile reception. The sponsor, however, was pleasant and surprisingly calm.

'We are indeed facing a number of technical issues, some of which are quite serious. But we trust that these will be overcome. What matters to us is that your people are taking the matter seriously. Every morning your project manager comes to my office at 8.30 a.m. She notes down all of my concerns and tells me how she plans to address them, either using her local organization, or by contacting technical experts elsewhere. At 4.30 p.m. she returns and updates me on the progress that has been made. In the IT business you rarely see a project without issues. I would not hesitate to work with you again on an innovative project with high risk. This is exactly the way I expect consultants to behave when there are issues in a project.'

Despite the severity of the issue, a positive perception had been maintained through the behaviour of the delivery team and their approach towards issue resolution.

Issues and transparency

We have emphasized the importance of good communication around the issue handling process, but the question arises as to the level of transparency that should be demonstrated. Should all issues, especially those that are internal, be raised with clients with the risk of damaging confidence?

Consider the following statements:

1. 'As consultants, our aim is to deliver both timely and accurate project outcomes, and an excellent client delivery experience.'

2. 'Raising an issue with a client demonstrates an honest and open approach, but may also create concerns and negative perceptions. We would therefore generally prefer to deal with internal issues behind the scenes.'

3. 'Clients expect a certain level of transparency, particularly if they will eventually be affected by an issue. Often the earlier that such information is communicated to the client the better. A good relationship is a no-surprises relationship.'

4. 'In some cases the optimal resolution to an issue may require client input. Without involving the client the use of such information to determine the optimal course of action would not be possible.'

Whilst all of these statements are true, they illustrate that managing client communication around issue handling requires good judgement. A delicate balance must be achieved to avoid communicating too much or too little. Whilst we have demonstrated that a lack of communication or action can have negative consequences, excessive communication may invoke unnecessary concerns.

'A commercial aircraft has many warning lights in the cockpit connected to the numerous technical systems operating on board. If every time a warning light illuminated the captain made an announcement informing his 200 passengers, there would probably be hysteria on flights every day. A warning light in a cockpit tells the pilot that he needs to take action. Minutes later the issue will usually have been resolved through the adjustment of flight controls or through the use of an auxiliary system. Only if the issue cannot be resolved and it is established that it will affect the progress of the flight is an announcement usually made.'

In the world of consulting a project manager has a similar choice to make. An internal issue that can be resolved relatively quickly and with high certainty can usually be handled as an internal matter without alerting the client. This is, however, an important judgement because later, if the consultants' attempts to resolve the issue are unsuccessful, it may turn out to have been advantageous to inform the client earlier in the process. This is clearly illustrated by the comments of a senior project manager working in the aviation industry.

'Last year I was responsible for supervising a project conducted by a consulting team for our organization. We had a mixed experience working with them. Whilst the quality of their work was good, their ability to make timely deliveries was somewhat haphazard. During the project we would ask them each week how the work was progressing and they would say that "everything was OK". At the end of the following week they would tell us again that "everything was OK". But then three days before the deadline everything would suddenly "not be OK" and they would advise us that we were facing a two-week delay. We found this frustrating. As a client we understand that issues come up in projects but we need better communication than this. If the consultants had approached us earlier we could have adjusted our plans to give them more time and also prepared our organization to absorb the delay with minimal impact.'

CHAPTER SUMMARY

The ability to deliver successful projects with a high degree of client satisfaction defines the calibre of a consulting organization.

- The 50:50 rule suggests that equal emphasis should be placed upon two elements: The provision of an accurate project result; and the delivery of a positive client experience. Consider the approach that you are applying in your work to excel at each of these things. What differentiates you from others, and in which of the elements is differentiation embedded?

- To produce accurate project results repeatedly and with high efficiency, consulting methodologies are often employed. A methodology generally consists of two components: A roadmap illustrating the steps required to navigate through the assignment; and a set of tools and templates that may be required along the way.

- A project organization will be required, tailored to the needs of the project and with clearly defined interfaces. Delivery resources may be located at the consultants' offices, on site, embedded in joint consultant–client teams or off-shore. Each of these approaches has its pros and cons.

- An internal launch meeting provides an excellent opportunity to assimilate the delivery team, brief them on the intended delivery strategy, answer questions and secure their commitment. Well-assimilated resources will make a more credible impact when interacting with clients.

- All consultants working at the client interface should consider themselves relationship managers and have choices as to the types of relationships that they build with their client counterparts. Once established, a partner-oriented relationship brings with it an improved understanding of the client organization, the potential for increased cooperation and often a degree of additional flexibility.

- A good client relationship must be maintained over time. Ensure that a consistent level of professionalism is

172 | ADDITIONAL TOPICS

demonstrated during day-to-day interactions, ensure that clients feel at ease through their confidence in your delivery approach, apply good judgement and keep clients updated at suitable intervals, and ensure that any questions or concerns are handled promptly.

- Dealing with issues during project delivery is a part of daily life in consulting. It is also something that consultants should be ready to approach with the correct mind-set and the issue-handling process should not be a dramatic one. Issues that arise may be internal and relate to processes within the consulting organization, or external and relate to the client organization or factors in the external environment. Some issues can be anticipated, whilst others arise unexpectedly. Depending upon the type of issue, different approaches can be applied and related communication with clients should be crafted carefully.

CHAPTER SEVEN

CLIENT INTERACTIONS AND RELATED OBSTACLES

A career in consulting brings with it the opportunity to work with a wide variety of client personnel at different organizational levels, representing different departmental functions. This can be a very rewarding experience in terms of personal growth, but also implies that consultants are required to build working relationships with a wide variety of people who have different personalities, backgrounds and agendas. This will require a degree of flexibility.

Clients can vary considerably in terms of style and approach: some may be formal and others informal; some may be well structured whilst others less structured; and some may be willing to collaborate openly whilst others may be more reserved. Clients may also have differing expectations of consultants, which will need to be understood and carefully managed. To accommodate these variables our approach will need to be sufficiently adaptable.

In Chapter 1 we described consulting as a *helping relationship*. However, in reality some people may be easier to help than others. Client-related obstacles can impact the value that we are able to deliver and must therefore be handled carefully. Some of the most common obstacles include poor client cooperation during the progress of an assignment, resistance when attempting to effect any kind of change, and conflicts of interest between stakeholders within a client organization.

Supported by examples, this chapter will explore practical strategies for dealing with these challenges.

THE IMPORTANCE OF ADAPTABILITY

The ability to work effectively with a broad range of stakeholders is an integral part of a consultant's role, but the adaptability required to achieve this is often underestimated. Small adjustments in one's own approach in response to the behaviours of client individuals or the culture of the client organization as a whole can result in significantly improved interactions. Experienced consultants know better than to walk in and do everything 'their way'. Instead they ask themselves how best to adapt their approach to succeed in the given situation. Furthermore, the approach that works well with one client may not work well with another. Figure 7.1 highlights some of the most common behavioural variables that may need to be considered in the fine-tuning of our approach.

Mature clients have a tendency to behave in a formal, well-structured manner and are concise in the way that they communicate. They also tend to have high expectations of consultants and expect us to be well prepared, well organized, and to deliver value at every point. Such clients may be either forthcoming in the sharing of information or reserved, sharing only limited need-to-know

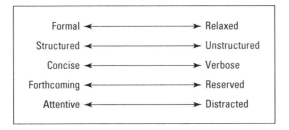

Figure 7.1: Common behavioural differences

facts. They may also put consultants to the test, expecting us to direct the dialogue and know the appropriate questions to ask.

A project conducted in the medical equipment industry involved a global vice-president as a client stakeholder. Meetings were always planned well in advance as it typically took four months to get a one-hour slot in her diary. Good preparation on all discussion points was essential, as the client would always be well prepared and would expect good answers to her questions. Meetings with this highly efficient individual were extraordinarily productive, and a clear position was generally achieved on each issue discussed.

Mature clients expect mature consulting behaviour. A casual or informal approach would have jeopardized the relationship with this client very quickly. During meetings it was important for the consultants to match the client's pace, to be well informed and to note down agreements accurately.

Another meeting was conducted with a public relations director in the pharmaceuticals industry. The client demonstrated a friendly and cooperative attitude, but with a highly verbose and social communication style. He loved to talk about football and started the meeting with a lengthy discussion about last night's game. During the meeting he provided good inputs based upon his specialist knowledge

> of the industry but with lengthy explanations, some of which were only loosely relevant to the discussion at hand, taking quite some time to get to the point.

In the fast-paced world of consulting, some consultants may find this type of behaviour frustrating. It is fair to say that what could have been accomplished in a 30-minute meeting with the first client would most probably have taken a full hour with the second. However, such variation is a reality, and a test of the consultant's ability to adapt. Being strict and to the point will not help you establish rapport with this type of client. Instead some patience will be required, as well as an ability to steer the discussion in a direction that will meet its objectives. Less relevant discussions about football may have to be tolerated periodically, before the discussion is diplomatically steered onto the next topic on the agenda.

Whilst some clients may be highly structured in their approach, others may be quite the opposite. This is again a test of the consultant's ability to direct the dialogue.

> A team was conducting a consulting project for a client in South America. The principal client stakeholder was highly skilled, passionate in her field and a creative thinker, but had a tendency to conduct herself in an unstructured and somewhat chaotic fashion. A short meeting scheduled with her to discuss four specific issues could easily last for more than an hour. During this time 20 different things could randomly be discussed without achieving a useful conclusion on any one of them.
>
> The consultants considered how they should adapt their approach to work efficiently with this individual. They ensured that prior to any meeting the specific discussion points had been agreed in the form of an agenda. Then as additional topics came up during the course of the meeting

they would respond: 'We have not included that point on the agenda for today. Is it something that should be added, or should we postpone the matter to a later discussion?' In some cases it was pertinent to amend the agenda, but usually the additional points were taken off-line.

Clients generally demonstrate attentive behaviours during meetings and presentations, but may sometimes be distracted by other matters. To ensure that meeting objectives are achieved, steps may be required to secure the required attention.

A consultant travelled from northern Europe to Italy to deliver a presentation to four managers in a client organization. The principle reason for making the trip in person rather than via teleconference was to build relationships, ensure good buy-in on the topics discussed and address any related concerns. As the consultant began his presentation he noticed that two of the participants were paying little attention, gazing into their phones, reading emails and sending messages. Concerned regarding the need to engage the managers, he adapted his approach by increasing the level of interaction with his audience. After presenting the short agenda he took his first check point. 'It is important for me to address your expectations', he said. 'Is this agenda complete for everybody?' Three participants nodded positively. The fourth was tapping an email into his phone. 'Mr De Luca, is the agenda fine with you?' he asked politely. 'Oh, yes', replied the fourth client, looking up. The presentation continued and a minute later the consultant engaged again with his next question. As the minutes passed the clients gradually put away their phones, realizing that this was not going to be the kind of meeting where they could do other work. In a one-way communication scenario it is easy for the listening parties to disengage, but when communication is two-way this becomes more difficult.

DEALING WITH CLIENT-RELATED OBSTACLES

Some of the most common client-related obstacles that we encounter as consultants relate to poor client cooperation, resistance to change and conflicts between stakeholders within the client organization.

Poor client cooperation

Consulting projects generally rely upon a certain level of cooperation with clients in order to achieve their outcomes. In some cases the client organization may, however, fail to provide the expected level of cooperation. This can arise for a number of reasons.

Client staff members may not appreciate the importance of the project and may not therefore be inclined to prioritize it. The managers within the client organization who engaged the consultants will most often not be the same people the consultants are required to work with on a daily basis. Client personnel may be thinking 'Why do we need to support this project? Why is it so important? It just sounds like additional work.'

One of the steps commonly taken to mobilize a client organization is to conduct a joint project launch meeting to get cooperation off to a good start. Scheduled after the internal launch meeting, this event is typically led by senior sponsors and the project managers from the client and consulting organizations. Senior sponsors present the business context of the project and explain its importance. The project managers outline the project approach, intended benefits and day-to-day working procedures that have been agreed. The meeting usually ends with a social event to initiate the process of relationship building.

Any project launch meeting should be viewed as a good opportunity to get everyone on the same page. Some of the content presented may be reused from the internal launch meeting, but other topics related to client-specific responsibilities may differ.

Give participants the opportunity to ask questions as it will be most efficient to answer them in a common forum. The building of a joint project team is an important objective of the meeting and this should be emphasized to the consulting team in advance if necessary. The example of poor practice below illustrates the type of behaviour that should be avoided.

> A project launch meeting involving 50 client and consulting staff members was conducted at an off-site conference facility. The event comprised a project presentation of one hour, a question-and-answer session of 30 minutes and a social activity where snacks and cocktails were served. When the social activity began the consultants had a tendency to congregate and chat on one side of the room whilst the client participants gathered on the other side, neither group interacting with the other. The sponsor within the consulting organization, alarmed by what she observed, immediately approached a number of her team members, leading them across the room and introducing them to their client counterparts.

Poor client cooperation may also occur when clients appreciate the value of the project but have insufficient time to support it due to other commitments and workload. In such situations it is important to make cooperation as easy as possible, demonstrating flexibility and a willingness to accommodate their schedules.

> A consultant was responsible for collecting status information from six client project managers at the end of each week. One project manager always provided his inputs late, delivered information that was incomplete and sometimes failed to submit his contribution at all. The manager concerned was responsible for a project that was running behind schedule and he was working long hours to try to resolve the situation. His time was in short supply and the reporting task ranked low among his priorities. The consultant

engaged with him to see if a solution could be found. 'Would it be helpful if I came to your office for a short meeting each week?' he asked. 'You could brief me and I could note down the status information. If your schedule is busy I could come in early and meet you at 8 a.m.' With the provision of this additional flexibility a working solution was agreed.

Client staff members may refuse to cooperate if they do not welcome the intervention of external consultants. There can be many reasons for this, including bad experiences that they have had working with consultants in the past. Relationships will be difficult to build with clients without willingness on both sides. In the following section we will therefore explore the phenomenon of resistance in some detail.

Resistance

Many consulting assignments are contracted to support the implementation of change within a client organization. The successful achievement of a client's vision may require changes to the organizational structure, the redesign of business processes, the implementation of new ways of working or the deployment of new support systems. Not everyone working in the client organization, however, may be open to change. Staff may not believe that the proposed changes will result in favourable outcomes; they may like the status quo and strive to preserve existing ways of working; conflicts of interest and political agendas may play a role; the use of external ideas may be resented, commonly referred to as *not-invented-here syndrome;* or some may believe that as a result of the changes their leverage within the organization will be compromised.

These feelings translate into *resistance* and a situation where client staff either refuse to cooperate during a project, or, even worse, take blocking actions to prevent progress within the assignment. The skill of dealing with resistance is important to any consultant and may, in some projects, make the difference between success and failure. In some situations we may encounter resistance that cannot be overcome, and the only way for a project to proceed is for client management to remove an individual who is blocking change from his or her position. This, however, is the extreme case, and the skilled and tactical handling of resistance is usually sufficient for project outcomes to be realized.

The approach for handling resistance does not have to be a complex one and begins with asking oneself the simple question 'Why?' Resistance is a natural human reaction and can have many possible causes. If we can identify the most probable causes then bringing down what is commonly referred to as the *wall of resistance* becomes a systematic process of addressing concerns. The better the concerns can be addressed, the lower the wall of resistance will become, but we must always start by attempting to establish the underlying cause. Consider the following example.

A consultant and his team were tasked to manage the implementation of a workflow system and associated business processes within a medium-sized company in Germany. The system would allow departments to exchange information electronically, eliminating a number of manual, paper-based processes and providing improved efficiencies. During the first week of the project the consultant arranged meetings with each of the departmental heads, important stakeholders whose people would be the users of the new system. His first meeting was with the head of the human resources (HR) department, a woman reputed to have strong opinions and little patience. He arrived at her office and knocked cautiously on the door, which was ajar. The manager glanced up. 'Oh!' she said in a stern voice. 'You must be the consultant, here about this new workflow thing that people are talking about!' The tone in her voice indicated clear disapproval.

'Yes', responded the consultant politely. 'I wondered if I could discuss the project with you. Could I have a few minutes of your time?'

'No', replied the manager without hesitation. 'We don't need a new workflow system here. We're doing just fine. Look at the pile of work on my desk. I am busy and we have plenty to do here. Go and talk to the people in the accounting department. All of the problems in this organization are in the accounting department. Goodbye!'

Consider how you would respond in this situation. Consultants have been known to react in a variety of ways, and with varying degrees of success:

- Some have simply argued, insisting, based upon their analysis, that a new system is required, but to little avail. No progress has been made and anything of a relationship that could have been built with the client has been eroded in the process.
- Some have attempted a selling exercise with words such as 'If you give me five minutes of your time I'm sure that I can explain how the new system will make your life much easier'. This approach is rarely successful with clients who are resistant and therefore unwilling to listen in the first place.
- Some have asked if they can make a new appointment at a more convenient time when the client is less busy. Sarcastic clients have told consultants on more than one occasion that they should come back next year, or in the next life!
- Others have emphasized the mandate for the project from senior client sponsors. 'We are sorry that you feel that

way; however, this initiative has been endorsed by your management and the project is already under implementation.' Be wary that even when management has made their endorsement, strong political influence many lie with other individuals in the organization. The client may simply respond: 'It's going to be implemented, is it? Well, we'll see about that!'

Let us now return to the fundamental question: Why? Answering this question is not an exact science and may even involve some guesswork. We do, however, have some clues to work with.

The statement 'We're doing just fine' implies 'Leave us alone. We don't want a new system forced on us.' The manager does not appreciate being told what to do in her department.

The statement 'We have plenty to do here' suggests that workload is already high and that staff have no time to worry about additional tasks, particularly if no associated benefit is perceived.

The most likely *causes* of resistance are therefore:

- An unwanted or forced intervention
- The prospect of additional time spent without tangible benefit. The solution to be implemented is probably perceived as a waste of time.

Any approach for handling the resistance will therefore need to:

- Acknowledge rather than challenge the client
- Associate value with the proposed system that is relevant, but without entering into selling mode.

The consultant did some quick thinking and responded. 'Very well,' he said. 'I am new to your organization, whereas you have been running this department for eight years, so I am sure that if anyone should be the best judge of whether or not you need a new system in HR it must be you.'

The client paused for a moment, having expected the consultant to argue. She responded in a more pleasant tone. 'Thank you.' The consultant sensed the invisible wall of resistance lowering slightly and felt the mood of the dialogue begin to soften.

He continued: 'But I have heard that in HR you do have a heavy workload, considering the number of people in your team. Workflow aside, would you have a few moments to share any other issues that you are facing, particularly ones that involve communication with other departments? I will be meeting the other departmental heads and an understanding of your views would be helpful.'

The client paused again, glancing at the pile of work on her desk. 'I really am very busy. But I suppose that just five minutes wouldn't hurt. Sit down,' she said, and began to explain. 'It's those people in the accounting department! They never send their figures to us on time. They are due by 4 p.m. every Friday and we usually get them at around 6 p.m. It's unacceptable! Then there are the backlogs. People do not fill out forms correctly. Everything has to be done twice and HR is blamed for the delays.'

The client continued to air her concerns for a few minutes before reaching a natural close. The consultant noted them down diligently.

'Thank you,' he said. 'This is helpful information. Tomorrow I will meet with the accounting department. Just out of interest, if they implement the proposed system in their department it will mean that you will always get the figures at exactly 4 p.m. The report will be produced by the system, irrespective of their actions. Would that be of help to you and your team?'

The client responded with a look of surprise. 'Can a workflow system really do that?'

A meeting that had started only minutes earlier with a poor outlook had resulted in a good consulting dialogue through the tactical handling of resistance. The client did not change her position on the workflow system overnight, but in continued discussions during the following days and through the strong commitment of the consultant to address her department's concerns she eventually become a strong supporter of the project.

As the example illustrates, the successful handling of resistance relies upon our ability to establish the most likely contributing causes. These causes clearly differ on a case-by-case basis. Consider a second example.

A manufacturing company in London had decided to replace its ageing accounting system. The system had been developed by the IT department within the company many years ago based upon an old technology. Mr Giles, the head of the IT department, and his team were responsible for maintaining the system and had customized it many times in response to changing requirements. Every time the marketing department wanted to implement a new invoice format or change the payment terms for a customer, his team would make the necessary changes.

The replacement of the system had now been agreed at management level. The two main drivers for this decision were to leverage some of the functions available in the latest accounting systems, and to enable integration with some of the other systems being used. Mr Giles had been put in charge of the project and a consulting firm had been engaged to support the selection and implementation of the replacement accounting system.

Following a structured methodology, the consultants collected requirements from both the IT and marketing departments, which were subsequently analysed. They then evaluated different systems available on the market and formulated a solution proposal. Finally, they arranged a meeting to present their recommended approach to the client. On the day of the meeting the marketing representatives were enthusiastic, but Mr Giles and his colleagues were not. They attacked the proposal at every opportunity, challenging assumptions, adding additional requirements and asking questions that the consultants would clearly not be able to answer without further investigation. The consultants acknowledged these concerns professionally and agreed to return the following week with an updated presentation. At the second meeting, however, Mr Giles and his team had come up with a list of new concerns. During subsequent meetings this continued and the consultants were forced to deal with additional points of criticism, time after time. As the weeks passed the marketing representatives became increasingly impatient as progress was slow and the new accounting system seemed to be a distant reality.

The manager responsible for the work in the consulting firm called an internal meeting with his team to discuss the situation. A lot of time and effort had already been expended, yet unless they were able to win the favour of Mr Giles it seemed that the project could not progress. The team gathered and asked themselves the fundamental question: why was this stakeholder so resistant to the proposal? During their discussion they reached the following conclusions:

- Mr Giles had been responsible for the development of the existing accounting system. He knew the system inside out, which was the source of great personal pride and made him something of an authority.
- The IT department was sitting on large budgets for the operation and maintenance of the existing system. These budgets would be reduced significantly once a new system had been implemented as support would be provided externally.
- The IT department were sitting in a powerful position. Each time marketing wanted to make a change they had to present a request to the IT department. They would evaluate the request and typically say 'We can do this, but it will take two weeks'. A new system would allow marketing to change invoice formats and payment terms themselves through a simple interface with little dependence on the IT department. 'Why did this used to take two weeks?' they would probably think.

In summary, whilst a new system would bring new features, lower costs and introduce integration possibilities to the IT department it also meant a dent in their pride, reduced budgets and loss of leverage within the organization. The most likely causes of the resistance had been established. An approach to address the resistance would need to:

- Acknowledge the merits of the existing approach, and ensure that the recommendation of a replacement system was not perceived as an attack on the work of the IT department

- Reinforce the importance of a replacement system to the business and the need to move ahead quickly, preferably with facts that would be hard to contradict
- Most importantly, put the IT department in the driving seat and demonstrate that the project could create a position of leverage for them.

Instead of scheduling another presentation for the following week, the consulting manager called for a meeting with Mr Giles and some of his senior team members.

'Mr Giles', he said, 'your team has been responsible for an accounting system that has served your organization well for many years. The proposal now to replace the system is intended to enable your company to compete more effectively in today's marketplace. A new system will allow you to offer customers flexible payment options, electronic invoicing and a number of other attractive features. Some of your competitors already have these capabilities, which underlines the need to act quickly. But it is your department that will own the new system, and it is ultimately your team that will make this a success. How can we as consultants support you in the best way?'

The discussion that followed during the meeting was much calmer in nature than those that had preceded it. The consultants emphasized their willingness to listen to concerns and discuss how they could be addressed. The role of the client's IT team and the importance of their involvement were also emphasized. It was a turn-around meeting that finally enabled the project to move forward.

Stakeholder conflicts

Conflicts between client stakeholders can create obstacles at various stages during a consulting engagement. Introduced earlier in Chapter 6, two approaches are commonly applied to address these conflicts: *facilitation* and *escalation*.

Facilitation

Assuming the role of a facilitator towards stakeholders within a client organization can help to navigate around obstacles and add value to the relationship as a whole. Consider the following example.

A conflict of interest existed between two client departments in Latin America concerning the definition of the scope and timeline for a project. The client's operations organization was pushing hard for an elaborate solution with many features to serve the company well in the long term. The client's marketing organization, on the other hand, wanted a lean solution that could be implemented quickly in order to support the launch of a new product. In discussions, each party complained that the other was unreasonable and a deadlock had resulted. The consultants responsible for collecting the requirements and providing the solution stepped in and attempted to facilitate. First, they engaged with the operations organization and persuaded them to divide the project into smaller phases with benefits delivered to the business incrementally. This meant that an elaborate solution could be delivered, but would also speed up the fulfilment of marketing requirements. Then they engaged with the marketing organization, explaining that certain operational requirements should be addressed early and it would be advisable to extend their requested timeline by 20% for the first delivery in order to accommodate this. The conflicting views of each department were facilitated into a window of reasonable agreement, and the project moved ahead.

In large corporations it is not uncommon to encounter departments with differing views, and that operate in a largely isolated manner. For matters where a common view is required, consultants are often in a good position to facilitate provided that they have established good relationships with the parties concerned. Clients often appreciate the value of such facilitation, particularly in long-term consulting relationships. This was echoed by a senior client manager in southern Europe:

> *'Our consulting provider has demonstrated the ability to engage with the different departments here, helping us to reach agreement and therefore speed up the decision-making process. It could be argued that we should not need this type of support from an external partner, but in practice we do, and it adds a lot of value.'*

Escalation

In some conflict-related situations facilitation may not be an option, or we may try to facilitate but without success. Agendas may be too diverse when figuratively one party wants black, one wants white and there is no grey, or lapses in cooperation may occur during project delivery that are beyond the influence of the consultants. In such situations escalation procedures will be required to engage stakeholders within the client organization who have sufficient authority to act and agree upon a resolution. When appointing a project organization it is important to define what are commonly referred to as *escalation paths* to ensure that these people can be accessed.

In the late 1990s a consulting team was engaged by the IT division of a telecommunications operator in eastern Europe to carry out systems development work. Whilst the team worked with the people in this organization on a daily basis they were required to obtain approval on all design documents by the client's marketing division. These two divisions worked in a somewhat isolated manner, communicating infrequently, and were physically located in buildings some distance apart. It was rumoured that the relationship between the two division heads was somewhat political.

As the first phase of the work drew to a close the consultants submitted their design documents for marketing approval but received no response. Reminders were sent, phone calls were made but days passed without progress. Finally, they escalated the matter to their client sponsor, the head of the IT department, asking for immediate action to avoid an inevitable project delay. His response came as something of a surprise. 'I'm sorry', he said, 'but I can't help you. If I call the head of marketing and he sees my number he does not pick up the phone.'

In this example two stakeholders with equal authority were unable to cooperate, but no escalation point had been defined one level higher in the organization with suitable rank to address the matter. The CEO of the client organization had not been defined as a project sponsor. It would have therefore been difficult and perhaps inappropriate for the consultants to try to involve him. Several weeks of delay resulted until the project could move ahead.

This situation is avoided by nominating senior sponsors as part of the project organization. These people will not necessarily attend regular project meetings, but their names will be listed on the project's organization chart. For strategic and high-visibility projects this is good practice from a leadership perspective but also creates an important safety net in case senior-level escalation is required.

Always ensure clear escalation paths are defined within the project organization. You may need them quickly in the event of poor cooperation during project delivery.

CHAPTER SUMMARY

Interactions with clients that are both efficient and effective are important enablers for the value that we can add as consultants.

- Successful consultants are expected to have the skills to work well with a wide range of clients. These clients may represent different organization levels, from top management to day-to-day operations, and bring different agendas. The importance of our ability to adapt to different behavioural styles and client expectations should not be underestimated.

- Poor client cooperation has been an issue that has negatively impacted many consulting projects at some point during their execution. Clients may be insufficiently motivated to provide the required cooperation, may have insufficient time available, or in some cases may simply be unwilling. Take steps to ensure the readiness of the client organization before a project begins and be ready to address any cooperation issues that occur.

- Consultants are engaged to effect change within client organizations, but those who do not support the changes are likely to view us as the enemy. In Chapter 1 we referred to consulting as a helping relationship, which suggests that when viewed as the enemy, a constructive consulting dialogue will be difficult to conduct. Our skills in handling resistance will therefore be instrumental to our ability to engage effectively.

- Resistance is a natural human reaction that requires a tactical approach. Take a step back and ask yourself the question: 'Why would this person feel resistant?' Use any available background information, but carefully observe client reactions during discussions. Handling resistance successfully is highly dependent upon your ability to address concerns.

- Conflicts between client stakeholders can create obstacles at various stages during a consulting engagement. Client facilitation can play a valuable role and can expedite the process of reaching practical agreements, but in some cases escalation may be required. Ensure that suitable escalation paths are in place as a safety net before project delivery begins.

CHAPTER EIGHT

THE SKILL OF ADVISING

There are many occasions during a consulting engagement when we advise our clients. Advice may be provided regarding the scoping of a problem and the definition of priorities; it may relate to the formulation of strategy, the design of a solution or an implementation approach; advice is shared on a daily basis as we provide answers to questions; it also has an important role to play internally within a consulting firm as we work in teams, supporting and sometimes challenging our colleagues.

The quality of the advice that we provide is driven by a number of factors. Our expertise, experience and ability to collect and analyse information play an important role, but we must also be skilled in combining these ingredients in the formulation of recommendations, supported by good arguments. These arguments must be defensible as clients often test our recommendations by challenging them. An argument that can be well defended is generally considered to represent good advice.

This chapter will explore techniques for building, presenting and defending arguments, supported by examples from real consulting engagements. The two most common systems of argumentation, *deductive* and *inductive* reasoning, will be introduced. We will also consider how arguments can be embedded in written documents and presentations.

THE DEDUCTIVE METHOD

The deductive reasoning method builds an argument using an analytical approach. Working from an initial *basis*, it eliminates sets of answers systematically until a unique conclusion is reached.

Building the argument

Consider the example below.

Sebastian has decided to buy a new car, specifically a sports utility vehicle (SUV). He consults a friend for advice who is familiar with the automotive industry, presenting the following requirements for the new vehicle:

- The car should run on diesel fuel.
- The car should have a sideward-opening rear door. Sebastian often needs to transport his golf clubs and wants the rear door to be easy to operate.
- He needs the car to be delivered within six weeks.

The friend carries out some analysis and presents the following recommendation shown in Figure 8.1.

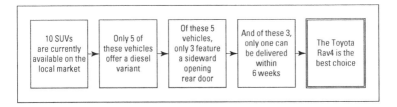

Figure 8.1: A deductive argument

A deductive argument builds from a solid basis or starting point. In practice this should be either a *fact* (something that can be observed or measured) or a *point of firm agreement* (something that has been agreed and will not be disputed by the receiver of the argument). The fact in this case is that only ten different SUVs are available in the local market. This is something that could be easily verified.

The argument then uses a funnel-type logic as illustrated in Figure 8.2. Having established ten possible options from its basis, each step in the argument uses information or *premises* to

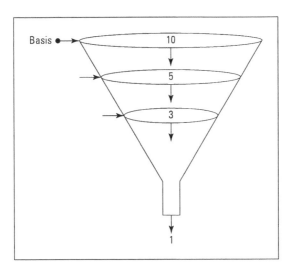

Figure 8.2: Deductive elimination process

eliminate sets of possible options and narrow down the number the potential choices.

A high-priority requirement for a diesel operated vehicle immediately reduces the number of possible options from ten to five. Upon further evaluation of these vehicles, two further models are eliminated due to the rear door opening mechanism. Finally, of the three vehicles that meet all other requirements only one can be delivered within the desired time frame. Provided that Sebastian agrees with the basis of the argument, hence its importance, and the reasons why other options have been eliminated, he should also agree with the final recommendation.

This is a simplistic example of a deductive process, and the elimination of options is rarely so clear-cut. Consider the following example, which requires the weighing of pros and cons prior to the elimination of options.

An on-line book retailer intends to implement a new order management system and has engaged consultants to identify a suitable choice. A workshop has been conducted to discuss the client's requirements. These requirements have been documented, verified and signed off by the client.

The consultants have conducted a quick look analysis, comparing the ten leading systems on the market with the client's requirements. A short list of three systems (A, B, C) has been defined, all of which are suitable choices to some degree.

Further evaluation has revealed that whilst system C meets all mandatory requirements, it offers lower performance than systems A and B and it has therefore been eliminated.

Systems A and B are both attractive choices and are priced at similar figures. System A offers more functionality, whilst

> system B offers greater expansion capability. The additional functionality offered by system A could be of interest in the future. Both systems offer adequate capacity and further expansion is unlikely to be required. System B is therefore eliminated and system A recommended as the optimal choice.

Whilst this example demonstrates the same type of logic, it uses as its basis a point of firm agreement with the client, instead of a fact. The client had reviewed the documented requirements and approved them.

Defending the argument

So far we have demonstrated that a deductive argument:

- Requires a solid basis
- Embodies a funnel-type logic
- Presents a unique conclusion through the elimination of alternatives.

Returning to our first example, now consider how the argument could be contested. There are two ways that a deductive argument can be overturned:

- The statements in a deductive argument act like links in a chain. If any one statement in the argument can be disputed and proven false, the chain will break and the conclusion may no longer hold. For example, if it can be proven that more than ten SUV options are available, and other options have not been considered; if in fact more than five vehicles offer diesel variants; if more than three vehicles feature sideward-opening rear doors; or if other vehicles can be delivered within the desired time frame.
- If any relevant information has been omitted, the argument could also be overturned. For example, another vehicle has an electrically operated tailgate, which would achieve the same convenience as the sideward opening rear door; it also complies with all the other requirements.

Two safety tests should therefore be applied before presenting a deductive argument:

- Can each premise be proven or reasonably substantiated?
- Has all relevant information been included?

If the answers to both of these questions is yes, then the argument can be considered robust.

THE INDUCTIVE METHOD

The deductive method of reasoning is analytical in nature, presenting a set of premises in a logical order to derive its conclusion. As the examples in this chapter suggest, analysis is often conducted to develop each premise within the argument and to ensure that it can be suitably substantiated.

The inductive reasoning method offers an alternative approach, which is more persuasive in nature. If anyone has ever said to you 'Give me five good reasons why...', you have probably responded with an inductive argument. Rather than presenting a chain of premises whose logical dependencies lead to a conclusion, the inductive method aggregates premises to demonstrate that its conclusion is likely to be true.

Building the argument

Consider the example in Figure 8.3. Unlike the deductive method, an inductive argument can accommodate the use of more subjective information, such as the statement 'It is popular' in Figure 8.3. Just because others like the car, there is no certainty that Sebastian will like it. The strength of an inductive argument relies upon the selection of good reasons that are well aligned with the receiver's priorities or decision-making criteria. The reason 'It is spacious' would, for example, carry no weight if the receiver was indifferent regarding the size of the car.

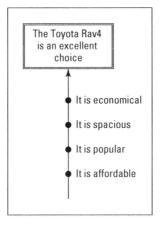

Figure 8.3: An inductive argument

Consider a second inductive example.

We recommend that you implement this system because:

- It meets all of your mandatory requirements
- It has strong references, thus minimizing risk
- The supplier can provide a local support team
- It is compatible with your existing environment
- It is within your budget.

This argument could be presented to a client, provided that each premise is valid and the premises are aligned with the client's decision-making criteria. In this case, minimizing risk and the local provision of support would need to be priorities for the client concerned.

Defending the argument

So far we have demonstrated that an inductive argument:

- Is built by aggregating multiple premises to support a conclusion
- Should contain premises that are relevant to client priorities
- Can accommodate information of a more subjective nature.

Returning to our first example, Sebastian could potentially contest any one of the statements:

- He may claim to know of other, more economical cars.
- He may need more space for additional luggage.
- The car may be popular elsewhere, but it is unfamiliar to him.
- The car may not be within his budget.

Consider the impact in each case. If the first statement in the argument holds, that is, Sebastian knows of other, more economical cars, then the recommendation would be weakened, but not necessarily destroyed. The argument has three other premises to rest upon, which together may still carry sufficient weight for the receiver. The same could potentially apply to the second and third statements. 'Given the other benefits of this car, is the luggage space really a deal-breaker?' one could ask. Sebastian may be willing to make a compromise. If the fourth statement holds, however, it would be quite likely to overturn the recommendation. Each premise is likely to have a different weight or priority to the receiver. If premises carrying sufficient weight can be disputed, or a fundamental criterion has been overlooked, then the argument is likely to fail.

> *When building an inductive argument we aim to identify a set of defendable premises that demonstrate completeness and are well aligned with the client's decision-making priorities.*

COMPARING THE METHODS

Two styles of reasoning have been introduced that differ both in style and in the quantity and quality of information required to build them. The greatest difference between the techniques, however, relates to the conclusions that they deliver:

- A deductive argument delivers, through analytical means, a conclusion that is *unique*. The first example in this chapter suggested that having analysed the available alternatives and the client's requirements, a particular vehicle was the *best* choice.
- The inductive argument, on the other hand, was simply building a case for a particular choice. Based upon the information presented, it argued that the vehicle was an *excellent* choice for the client, but it is not exhaustive.

This important distinction affects the application of the argumentation methods in practice, as illustrated by the example below.

A global engineering group comprised five businesses with facilities in different locations, dedicated to the manufacture of specialist automotive equipment. At each facility a system was used to manage inventory in a large warehouse where parts were stored. A different system was in use at each location, which had been identified as a source of inefficiency by management. A decision had therefore been taken to purchase a common system so that all facilities could benefit from shared operational costs.

A team of consultants had been engaged to support the selection of the replacement system and began their assignment by collecting requirements from each of the five businesses. As expected, whilst some of their requirements were similar, others were not. Some businesses insisted on the inclusion of requirements that would be redundant to others, and some other requirements were very specific to working practices within a particular facility.

The consultants evaluated a number of commercially available systems to identify an option suitable for group-wide use. Whilst a system was identified that represented the best fit overall, it could not be described as an ideal fit in each individual case. Three of the businesses would be the greatest benefactors as all of their requirements would be satisfied. The other two businesses would lose some features existing in their current systems. These features were non-critical but would require certain working processes to change, and the consultants anticipated some resistance when presenting their proposed solution. It could be argued that these two businesses would have been better off continuing working with their existing systems, but this would defeat the objective of the initiative as a whole. The consultants considered how they would approach the presentation of their recommendation.

The stakeholders in each business had agreed to move to a common system provided that their requirements were satisfied. For the first three businesses this objective had been achieved. A deductive line of reasoning could therefore be used, as illustrated below:

- Our analysis has identified three systems that are compliant with your mandatory requirements: X, Y, Z.
- System X has lower performance than Systems Y and Z. It has therefore been eliminated.
- Of the two remaining systems, System Y would take more time to implement due to poorer compatibility with the other systems that you are currently using. It has also therefore been eliminated.

We have therefore identified System Z as the best option for you to proceed with.

For the other two businesses, however, this line of argumentation would not hold. System Z was not the best choice for them and their stakeholders would recognize this immediately. An inductive line of reasoning was therefore used to recommend the implementation of System Z:

- It satisfies most of your mandatory requirements.
- For requirements that are not satisfied we can recommend work-arounds through changes to your working processes.
- You will benefit from reduced operational costs.
- It is in the interest of the group as a whole to use a common system.

The last premise in this argument uses what is referred to as the *greater good argument*. In cases where the needs of all stakeholders cannot be satisfied by a recommendation it refers to overriding benefits to the organization as a whole as the basis for making a compromise.

COMBINING THE METHODS

When addressing complex situations, several arguments may be needed to support different parts of a recommendation. These parts could include the definition of priorities, the selection of solution options, the choice of deployment approach, and so forth. To support this, arguments can be combined in the form of layers, each contributing to the strength of the overall recommendation. Consider the following example.

TransCom is a company working in the media business. Already operating in four countries, it has stated a vision to be ranked as a leader in its local markets within three years. Having engaged with TransCom in several meetings, Dasser Consulting is preparing a proposal to help bring this aim about. The proposal will focus on the client's vision, current position and the contributions that Dasser could provide as consultants. The main argument to be embedded in the proposal is illustrated in Figure 8.4.

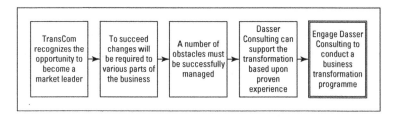

Figure 8.4: The proposal: main argument

The style of deductive reasoning employed in this argument differs somewhat from the examples presented earlier in this chapter, yet with many similar characteristics.

- The argument begins with a basis that must be solid.
- Each premise either draws a conclusion from the previous one, or makes a comment that will help to reach a conclusion.
- All relevant information must be included for the argument to be intact, and each premise must be substantiated.

Having formulated the main argument, the Dasser team adds a second layer of arguments, based upon analysis that they have carried out (Figure 8.5). Here, inductive arguments have been added to substantiate each premise:

- The opportunity for TransCom to become a market leader is substantiated by new opportunities created by changes in regulation, rapid growth in TransCom's markets, business opportunities presented by emerging customer segments, opportunities to partner with other firms, and the potential leverage their existing customer base.

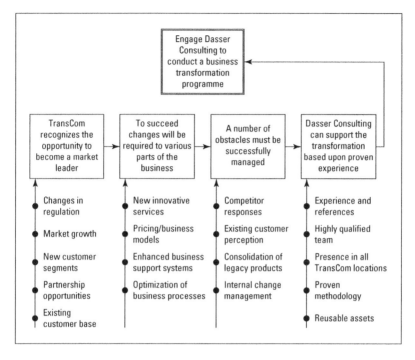

Figure 8.5: The proposal: second-level arguments

- The main changes that will be required to the business are summarized and relate to service innovation, the need for new pricing and business models, additional functionality in business support systems and the need to optimize operational processes.

- The actions proposed to manage obstacles relate to the formulation of strategies to deal with competitor responses, the management of existing customer perceptions, the consolidation of legacy products and a structured approach towards internal change management.

- Finally, to justify Dasser's suitability as a partner, material has been prepared concerning their references, the calibre and geographical placement of their consulting resources, their proven transformation methodology, and the assets that they could contribute for reuse.

Inductive arguments are well suited for use at the detailed level. If any detailed finding came into dispute, the argument would be weakened but is less likely to be overturned, enabling it to continue to support the main deductive argument.

DOCUMENTING THE ARGUMENT

The Dasser team intends to embed the argument into a written proposal document. The structure of the argument lends itself well to this, as illustrated in Figure 8.6. The document's executive summary is created by elaborating on the premises of the main argument in the following way:

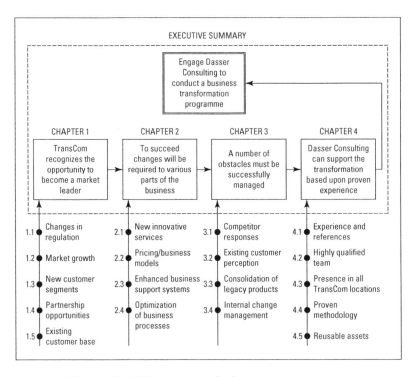

Figure 8.6: The proposal: document structure

Executive summary

TransCom has recognized an opportunity to become a leader within the next three years in the markets in which it operates.

The successful achievement of this will require changes in several areas of the business: New innovative services will be required to create differentiation from competitors; flexible pricing and business models will be required to attract, in particular, profitable enterprise customers; business support systems will need to be enhanced to provide new capabilities; and operational processes must be optimized in order to deliver the required levels of speed and efficiency.

A number of obstacles must also be successfully managed: strategies to deal quickly with competitor responses will be required; existing customer perceptions will need to be influenced to prevent customer churn; legacy products will require consolidation; and internal changes must be facilitated skilfully.

Dasser Consulting brings substantial experience of supporting business transformations in the media industry, illustrated clearly by our references and the testimonials of our clients. We have teams of specialists located at all TransCom locations, employ a highly developed methodology to ensure the success of our projects, and can bring a number of reusable assets to bear. These, among other factors, position us as an ideal consulting partner for this assignment.

The table of contents outlining the remainder of the document is also derived from the argumentation structure, and is illustrated in Figure 8.7. Each main premise is translated into a chapter within the document, whilst premises of the second-level arguments become sections within each chapter. Through the addition of good documented content within each section, supported by analysis, charts and diagrams, a strong proposal is developed that is well argued at every point.

A similar approach is employed when preparing a set of presentation slides to be presented to the executives at TransCom. Figure 8.8 illustrates the outline of the presentation.

Each premise in the main argument has been translated into a presentation slide or group of slides to cover the content of the second-level premises. The number of slides required in

EXECUTIVE SUMMARY

CHAPTER 1 – A Potential Market Leader: TransCom's Opportunity
1.1	Changes in Regulation
1.2	The Market Forecast
1.3	Emerging Customer Segments
1.4	Opportunities to Partner
1.5	Leverage of Existing Customer Base

CHAPTER 2 – Proposed Activities: A Focused Approach
2.1	New Service Innovation
2.2	Pricing and Business Models
2.3	The Role of Business Support Systems
2.4	Speed and Efficiency through Process Optimization

CHAPTER 3 – Obstacles to be Managed
3.1	Anticipated Competitor Moves
3.2	Existing Customer Perceptions
3.3	Consolidation of Legacy Products
3.4	Organizational Change Approach

CHAPTER 4 – Dasser: A Transformation Specialist
4.1	Success through the Application of Experience
4.2	A Team of Specialists for TransCom
4.3	Engagement at Global and Local Levels
4.4	Our Proven Methodology
4.5	Reusable Assets

Figure 8.7: The proposal: table of contents

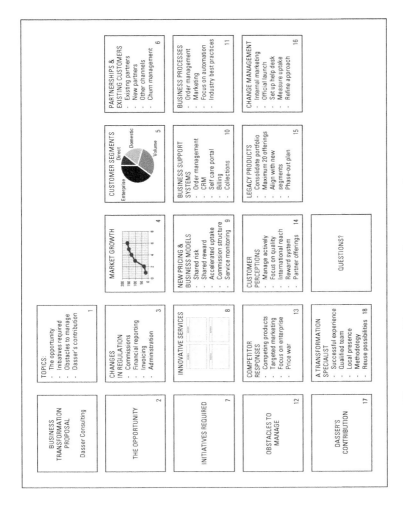

Figure 8.8: The proposal presentation structure

each group varies according to the amount of content to be presented. As the slides are presented, the logic of the overall argument will therefore be maintained.

PRESENTING AN ARGUMENT

Before presenting an argument in the form of a presentation, good preparation will be required. Pay particular consideration to the following points:

1. Make sure that you have a clear understanding of the arguments in your presentation and the information that supports them. This will help you to deliver a clear and convincing message.
2. Decide on your approach for narrating your presentation slides. Select any supporting examples or anecdotes that you plan to use during your delivery.
3. Anticipate the questions that your audience is likely to ask and prepare good answers. Often, additional presentation slides are prepared if needed to support the answering of specific questions. These slides are only shown if the questions arise, but demonstrate a robust and well-prepared approach.
4. Think about damage control. The recommendations that consultants present may represent bad news to some stakeholders, and they may raise objections when the presentation is delivered. Decide how these objections will be handled and how concerns will be addressed.

A well-presented argument should develop the understanding of the audience incrementally as it is delivered. To ensure that this is achieved, select appropriate points to check in with the audience and ensure that everyone is on board. Any questions or concerns should be addressed before proceeding to the next step in the argument, and generally the sooner this is done, the better.

Consider also the composition of the audience that you are addressing. Consultants have made the mistake of delivering the same presentation slides to several different departments within an organization and have had greater success with some departments than others. Your presentation will need to be adjusted to address the specific needs and interests of each audience that you engage with, in order to secure a high level of commitment. This may require the addition of details for the benefit of some audiences that will not be presented to others.

CHAPTER SUMMARY

The skill of advising is fundamental to a consultant's role. Good advice supported by clear argumentation will win the respect of clients and colleagues alike. This chapter has introduced the two fundamental building blocks for building arguments, the deductive and inductive reasoning methods.

- The deductive method is analytical in nature and presents a set of premises that act like links in a chain arriving at a therefore-type conclusion. Two safety tests should be applied when validating this type of argument: Has all relevant information been included? Can each statement be substantiated?

- The inductive method is more persuasive in nature and aggregates premises to suggest that its conclusion is likely to be true. For an inductive argument to be strong, ensure that the selected premises are well aligned with client priorities and decision-making criteria.

- When formulating more complex recommendations, several arguments may be needed and are subsequently layered. The main argument creates the backbone of the recommendation and often takes the most time to perfect. Supporting arguments are built based upon information and analysis that justify each premise in the main argument, ensuring that the recommendation is intact. A well-structured argument should be easy to embed in a report, proposal or presentation.

- Once an argument has been prepared it must be presented to the client, and in many cases defended. In preparation for strong presentation delivery, review the main arguments, prepare a suitable narrative, anticipate potential questions and consider damage control in advance if necessary.

ADDITIONAL REFERENCE
MATERIAL

Good luck implementing the ideas presented in this handbook! Readers can access additional consulting tips as an extension to those provided in this book at:

www.spconsulting.se/TCH

Samir Parikh and his team regularly conduct seminars on the topic of consulting for corporations that aim to transform themselves into consulting-based organizations in order to improve their competitive edge.

INDEX

NOTES

NOTES

NOTES

NOTES

Printed and bound by CPI Group (UK) Ltd, Croydon, CR0 4YY

13/04/2025

14656556-0001